Pizitz

YOUR STORE

TIM HOLLIS

Charleston — London

THE
History
PRESS

Published by The History Press
Charleston, SC 29403
www.historypress.net

Copyright © 2010 by Tim Hollis
All rights reserved

First published 2010

Manufactured in the United States

ISBN 978.1.59629.993.1

Library of Congress Cataloging-in-Publication Data

Hollis, Tim.
Pizitz : your store / Tim Hollis.
p. cm.
Includes bibliographical references.
ISBN 978-1-59629-993-1
1. Pizitz (Department store) 2. Department stores--Alabama--History. I. Title.
HF5465.U64P594 2010
381'.14109761781--dc22
2010036488

Contents

ACKNOWLEDGEMENTS

When The History Press first approached me about assembling the history of the Pizitz stores, I was most grateful that it was a subject I had already been researching for several years. The story has been touched on in some of my previous books on Birmingham nostalgia, but I knew that if I were going to tell the story properly, I would need to go deeper than I had ever gone before.

The names that follow are those individuals whose contributions most resulted in the book's final format. Some of them provided their help many years ago; in fact, several of these people are no longer with us to see this final product. Therefore, for all their help, both past and present, I would like to thank:

Jim Baggett
Jess Bullock
Rich Campbell
Earle Cappellen
Beth Clayton
Irby Cohen
Allene Bridgman Colvin
Charles Elliott
Jeremy Erdreich
Leigh Ferguson
Heather Flaherty

ACKNOWLEDGEMENTS

Joe Floyd
B.J. Goldstein
Martha Haarbauer
Kurt Hertrich
Ann Knight
Ernest Langner
Jo Lawley
Jim and Carolyn Luker
Sylvia Martin
Tiny Muse
Merritt Pizitz
Michael Pizitz
Richard Pizitz
Susan Pizitz
Sharon Hamrick Slawson

They've all got style…they've got Pizitz!

Chapter 1

THE PEOPLE'S STORE
ON THE BUSY CORNER

It is accurate to say that for the eighty-seven years the Pizitz department stores were part of life in Alabama—and Birmingham in particular—they owed much of their character to the personality of their founder. The fact that the chain managed to remain under family ownership, rather than that of a parent corporation, ensured that the stores could never stray too far from their roots. Those roots began with Louis Pizitz.

Fortunately for the cause of future historians, Louis lived long enough to become a local legend in Birmingham, and befitting his status, the major events of his life were well documented—if sometimes simplified and condensed—in numerous interviews and newspaper articles over the years. Our most complete account of his early life comes from Louis himself, who sometime during the 1950s was prompted to sit down and compose a document telling his own story. Since obviously there is no living person who was a firsthand witness to these events, this is the nearest we can hope to get to hearing it from someone who was there. Louis wrote:

> I was born in BrestLitovak, Poland, on April 3, 1867. My father was in the leather business. He was not rich but pretty well off and well-to-do. We had our own home and own store and a few thousand rubles in the bank. My father died when I was five years old and my mother died when I was seven years old. I had one brother and three sisters.

I went to a Hebrew school and when I was fifteen years old I went to a Hebrew college and stayed there until I was seventeen years old. Then I left college and went to work.

Although Louis did not elaborate on his college days, his biographers later determined that he was studying to become a rabbi. Any particular reason he might have had for abandoning this career choice in favor of business has not been recorded with any certainty, but in any event, we now resume Louis's own story:

I went to Bialystock and went to work for a concern that made shoddy [a coarse woolen material]. I stayed with them about three years. They paid me 50 rubles a week and I had charge of five hundred people. I was less than twenty years old. I saved up a thousand rubles and went in partners with another man. We bought 10 carloads of shoddy and in order to save money, we had it shipped in open cars. We bought this on September 25, and the snows were so big that it did not reach Bialystock until January 25, and it was all ruined. I owed the bank 14,000 rubles, which I could not pay, so I left and came to this country.

Again, someone helping write the story of Louis's life later pinpointed his arrival in the United States as taking place in September 1889. Louis was probably not in the mood to look at the calendar to see the date anyway, because as he recounted:

When I reached New York, I did not have a dollar and walked around the streets for three days, sleeping in the park and eating garbage on the streets. I met up with a woman, a Mrs. Frank, from Augusta, Georgia. She was from my same town in Poland, so she wanted to help me. She said she had peddlers' supply of goods in Augusta and took me home with her and gave me some jewelry to peddle. I carried a pack on my back for two and a half years. In this time I saved up $750.

Apart from his autobiography, from which we have been quoting so far, at some point Louis gave another interview in which he elaborated on a definite handicap during his door-to-door peddler days in Georgia: namely, that he did not speak English.

The fact that I was unable to speak the language was, of course, one of my greatest drawbacks. But I made signs to my customers and occasionally learned a word of English as an aid. At night, I spent many hours poring over my books by a coal oil lamp in my efforts to master the English language. It was rather a hard job, but then if your living depends upon knowledge of how to speak the language, you will soon learn.

His immediate family confirms that for the rest of his life, Louis spoke English with a heavy Polish accent that would have convinced no one that he learned the language in the Deep South. Getting back to Louis's writings, we pick up his story with the money he managed to save during the years he was peddling his wares:

I took the $750 and went to Swainsboro, Georgia, and opened up a little store. I paid eight dollars a month rent, not in money but in merchandise. While in Swainsboro, I married and in five years I saved or made about $50,000. My wife said if I could do that in a little town, I could do much better in a city. She was not satisfied in Swainsboro and insisted that I look for some city to go to. We were the only Jews in Swainsboro at that time, and it was a very small town with no lights, no water or conveniences, and my wife insisted I leave.

Louis's wife, who figures prominently in his story both above and below, was the former Minnie Smolian, whom he married in 1891. We have often heard the cliché that behind every successful man is a woman, and this seems particularly true when it came to getting Louis to move to what would become his adopted home city:

I traveled around looking at several places and finally decided to try it in Birmingham, Alabama. I had about $11,000 in cash and the balance of the $50,000 in merchandise and accounts due. When I left Swainsboro, I turned my store over to Mr. Erhlich to run.

When I started out in Birmingham, the population was 27,000. I rented a small store on 23rd Street and First Avenue for $75 a month rent, and was scared to death that I could not pay this much rent. I stayed there about four months and did nothing. I had some merchandise I had brought over from Swainsboro, but it would not sell here.

At that time, Ferd Marx was on the corner where my store is today. He moved over to a store next door to the Caheen Brothers and I took over the

**2026
First Avenue**

Bet. 20th and 21st Streets.

Louis Pizitz's

New Store

Opened To-day

8 A. M.

Brim Full of Bargains.

THE PEOPLE'S STORE.

Dry Goods,

Clothing,

Shoes and

Men's Furnish'gs

Newest Goods!

Correct Styles!

Goods for All Classes!

A Few of Our Extraordinary Inducements for this---Our Opening Week.

Compare Prices.

Every piece of goods in my store marked down for this, my opening week. New and direct from the factory.

corner and paid $100 a month rent. I stayed there two months and did nothing. I was disgusted and wanted to go back to Swainsboro, but my wife insisted that I keep trying. I did business with the Birmingham Trust Company, so I went over to see them to borrow $1,500. I had a hard time getting it. I made up my mind that I would lose it and everything I had, and then my wife would want to go back to Swainsboro.

Now that we have heard Louis's chronology of how it all happened, let us peek at the crumbling newspapers of the era—fortunately preserved on microfilm before they disintegrated completely—and see what more they can tell us. An ad in the *Birmingham News* of March 15, 1899, tells us that "Louis Pizitz's New Store Opened Today" at an address of 2026 First Avenue (further pinned down as between Twentieth and Twenty-first Streets). Is this the same original store that Louis said was at First Avenue and Twenty-third Street? Possibly—but he also said that he spent four months at that location while doing no business.

Scarcely three weeks after the "new store" ads ran, on April 5, the ads read, "Change of Location: L. Pizitz Permanent Location, Corner 19th Street and Second Avenue, Ferd Marx's Old Stand." Ferd Marx, a pioneer in Birmingham's department store trade, had vacated those premises on January 23 to move to a spot in the next block of Second Avenue. (That Ferd Marx building would later become

This advertisement appeared in the *Birmingham News* on March 15, 1899. Was this the opening of Louis Pizitz's very first store in Birmingham? There seems to be no evidence to indicate otherwise, even though the location and timing do not agree with Louis's later recollections of how his business began. *Author's collection.*

Birmingham's first Woolworth's store, in 1940 a Walgreen's drugstore and later Mangel's department store.)

So, we do know that April 5, 1899, was the day the Pizitz store arrived at its final destination. Was there actually another First Avenue store that opened before the one on March 15? If so, it was not advertised in the months preceding that. Of course, if business was so bad, perhaps Louis did not have the money to place newspaper advertising—or maybe the lack of business made those three weeks seem like four months to him in retrospect. There is also the possibility that in dictating this story to some anonymous stenographer later, Louis could have said "four months" when he meant "four weeks." At any rate, in future years the Pizitz store always calibrated its anniversaries based on an April 1899 founding, for whatever historical value that is worth. We are left with two possible scenarios, but at least they both end up with the store in its well-known location.

It would seem that one influence on Louis's decision to make it or break it in Birmingham was the comparatively recent success of another immigrant merchant. In 1870, Adolph B. Loveman, a former shepherd from Hungary, opened a small store in Greensboro, Alabama, and by 1887 saw enough promise in the sixteen-year-old Birmingham to move his business there. Over the next few years, he took on two partners, M.V. Joseph and Emil Loeb, and the name of the business became Loveman, Joseph & Loeb (later to be known simply as Loveman's).

In 1890, the firm bought a piece of property at the corner of Third Avenue and Nineteenth Street that would end up being its home for the next ninety years. Between 1890 and 1900, the building continued to grow and expand until it occupied almost a quarter of that entire city block. By the time Louis Pizitz arrived in the neighborhood, Loveman, Joseph & Loeb was advertising itself as "the largest store south of the Ohio," which could have well been true. The success of Loveman's must have been particularly irritating to Louis as he seemingly spun his wheels trying to make a go of his own store. It might not have occurred to him at the time that he would eventually become Loveman's biggest competitor, but things soon began to turn around. Again, here is how Louis explained it:

> *The first thing I started selling good was domestic at three cents a yard when everybody else was selling it for five cents. I sold nothing but bargains and I commenced to do business and to make money. I give all the credit for my success to Jim Pughley, who was helping me then. He is in Lyons, Georgia, now. I made money from then on and bought out the*

three other stores in that block. There was a saloon on the corner. I would buy one store at a time.

Once the Pizitz store began catching on with the public, there was no stopping it. Those first newspaper ads in March 1899 featured the slogan "The People's Store," and shortly thereafter the logo that was plastered all over its advertising became simply "Your Store." Louis Pizitz seemed to have a particular affinity for the common man, probably because it had not been very long since he himself had been in a rather dire condition. This attention to the needy would win Louis, and by extension his business, loyal customers for generations.

Years later, Louis's son Isadore gave a reporter some insight into his father's philosophy: "Dad always preached about treating the customer right. He said you can never fool a customer. Just try it...mix some poorly-made stuff in with your good merchandise, then stand back and watch. The customers will sort it much faster than you can."

This portrait of Louis Pizitz was obviously made later in his life, but it was one of the most often-published images of the downtown merchant. Photos of the much younger Louis, with black hair and mustache, often appeared in newspaper ads, but unfortunately none of those are of sufficient quality for reproduction. *Author's collection.*

"Dad also said that your executives and buyers can't make great," Isadore went on. "The heart of the business, he'd say, is your salespeople and the other employees who deal with the public. They're the ones who make a store."

Another associate, E.M. Danenberg, told the same reporter:

> *He was quite a merchant, but he was a doggone good human being, too. He spoke a kind of broken English, but you never had any trouble understanding what he wanted.*
>
> *One day, he walked through just as I'd sold a customer a nice pair of trousers. He stopped and rubbed the material between his fingers and said, "That's good merchandise you're buying there!" Then, loud enough so I could hear, he added, "You need nice BELT go with those trousers…"*

Louis's legendary reputation extended far beyond the walls of his store building, and it grew just as exponentially as that structure. The story has often been told how, when thousands of Alabama coal miners had gone on strike for better working and living conditions, Louis sent food and clothing to the impoverished mining camps by the truckload. Some mine operators chose to shut down their mines in an attempt to starve their striking employees out, but Louis bought some of these idle mines and put the workers back on the job just so he could sell the coal at cost.

Another of his philanthropic efforts was described thusly in another of his many biographies: "When the cotton market collapsed in 1914, he advised farmers not to sell at 11 cents per pound, a price below cost of production. Pizitz made loans at 15 cents per pound, storing the cotton until prices went back up with the United States' entry into World War I."

While helping anyone and everyone he could with his philanthropy, Louis never neglected his own religious heritage. In his autobiography, he wrote:

> *The main thing in my life that I am glad of more than anything else is that I started the Young Men's Hebrew Association in Birmingham. They had a lot on 17th Street and 8th Avenue and were in debt for street improvements and taxes in the amount of $2,500. I paid the $2,500 myself and then started a building fund. I gave $10,000 to start this and we got a new building. I thank God for this, and now they have a beautiful building and over $200,000 in cash for a larger building.*
>
> *Our synagogue on 7th Avenue was strictly Orthodox, and I thought for the young people they ought to have a synagogue between the Orthodox and*

the Reformed, so I gave $10,000 to start a fund to build a new synagogue. I thank God that we now have one of the finest synagogues of any place in the South.

But like his other charitable work, Louis did not let his own religion or anyone else's get in the way wherever he was needed. He wrote:

In 1917 the Catholic Committee came to me and asked me to be chairman of a committee to raise $75,000, and I raised over $150,000. The Catholic organization was so pleased they gave me a big banquet and a silver loving cup, which is engraved "General Louis Pizitz." At the big banquet, Judge Grubb and his wife kissed me, and then I never was kissed so much in all my life. I will never forget all the women who kissed me. The City of Birmingham wanted to give me a loving cup and I refused to accept this, which was very foolish and I have been sorry ever since that I would not take it.

While recognition was being heaped upon Louis from all sides, his store kept growing and spilling over, not unlike a washing machine into which a novice homemaker had dumped a whole box of soap powder. A postcard from the late 1910s—one of the only views of the Pizitz corner from that era—shows the signage for the Louis Pizitz Dry Goods Company, as it was called by that time, covering at least two or three buildings of widely varying architecture and uneven size. In fact, a slogan that rivaled "Your Store" for sheer ubiquity in the ads designated the store's location as "the Busy Corner." As Louis wrote, he had to continue acquiring more property to keep up with the business:

In 1917, I had a million dollars in merchandise and cash, and mostly in money. I bought out two stores and in 1918 I bought out the corner from Mr. Smith and paid him $325,000 in cash. Then I bought the next piece, 40 feet, for $190,000. I then had 140 feet on 19th Street and 100 feet on Second Avenue. Then I bought the next two pieces on Second Avenue for $90,000.

In 1920, I got an architect to make up plans for my new building. I thought the building would cost me all together a million dollars. I built it in two sections. The first building cost me nearly $900,000. I borrowed a million dollars from Metropolitan Life Insurance Company for this and went back later and borrowed $500,000 more to build the corner building, which cost me $675,000.

Right: Once the first portion of the new seven-story Pizitz store had been completed, the employees presented Louis Pizitz with this bronze plaque. Notice that even at that early date, they had the founding date off by a couple of years. *Pizitz family collection.*

Below: This rare photo was probably taken in June 1924. Notice that at far right, the first half of the seven-story addition had apparently been completed, but the original structure at Second Avenue and Nineteenth Street was still drawing crowds and justifying its signage as "the Busy Corner." *Pizitz family collection*

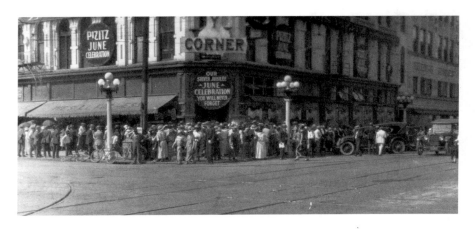

Surviving photographs uphold Louis's account that the present-day Pizitz building was constructed in two sections. The original part of the seven-story structure was the westernmost part facing Second Avenue, which was apparently occupied for the first time in 1923. Demolition of the original corner building was underway by January 1925, and the remainder of the seven-story building was completed and imperceptibly connected to the 1923 building sometime later that year. One would think that the newspaper advertisements would help pinpoint the exact date, but such is not the case. There are hints, though. That was the era when department store ads relied on text even more than graphics, and one blurb published on September 1, 1925, signed by Louis himself, explained his retail philosophy:

> *I have faith in Birmingham. I have faith in you. I have shown my faith by investing all my life's earnings in a building for you. I have faith in my buyers and their buying. I have faith in my merchandise. I have faith in my organization. I have faith that you, the Birmingham public, will support this wonderful institution, built with the vision of a greater Birmingham.*

By the time of this February 1925 photo, the original "Busy Corner" building had been demolished, and work was about to begin on the other half of Pizitz's mammoth store building. When it was finished, the brick wall seen on the existing seven-story portion was knocked out, and the two halves joined together seamlessly. *Pizitz family collection.*

This September 1925 newspaper page was typical of Pizitz's advertising style of the era. Although it does not specifically mention the new addition to the store, in the fine print Louis tried to make the citizens of Birmingham feel at least a little guilty if they did not patronize his business: "I have shown my faith by investing all my life's earnings in a building for you." *Author's collection.*

If it sounds a bit like Louis was trying to make shoppers feel guilty if they did not visit his new building—well, let's just say that the precarious financial arrangements he described above could have had a lot to do with that. Now Louis Pizitz had an impressive monolith of a department store rising seven stories above the sidewalk below, dwarfing the old Loveman, Joseph & Loeb building in the next block. The only thing separating the two competitors was the Louis Saks department store, which had been built on the site of the Florence Hotel in 1916. (Many people, seeing period photos, have misinterpreted the name and thought Birmingham once had a branch of New York's famed Saks Fifth Avenue store. The Saks that stood like a referee between combatants Pizitz and Loveman's was strictly a locally owned affair, however.) In the fashion of the day, only the two sides of Pizitz that faced

Once the entire store building was completed, no one could have detected that it was built in two parts. Just in case anyone had missed Pizitz's slogan as "Your Store," it was spelled out in huge neon letters on the two sides that faced the streets. *Author's collection.*

Second Avenue and Nineteenth Street were finished with their elaborate terra cotta surfacing. The southern and western walls were left unadorned, but since they towered over the surrounding cityscape, the topmost portion of each was painted with a huge mural spelling out the Pizitz name.

The view from Pizitz's seventh floor might have looked like everything was finally in the clear in the late 1920s. As Louis was about to learn, though, fate was not quite finished with him yet. The trials that were about to come would threaten to sink his business once more—only this time, there would be an entire nation in the same leaky boat with him.

Chapter 2

DEFEATING THE DEPRESSION WITH DOLLY DALE

S ome wise guy once quipped that the Great Depression hit the United States at a most inopportune time—just when so many people were out of work. But seriously, folks...

The events that followed the stock market crash of October 1929 were enough to test the mettle of every person in the country, but when a person had recently borrowed money for a building program the size of the Pizitz store, it made things look even more hopeless. From his more comfortable perch of the 1950s, Louis Pizitz recalled how he was so desperate that he wanted the entire business taken off his hands:

> *I did pretty well in business until 1929. I owed Metropolitan Life Insurance Company a million and a half dollars at 5½ percent interest, and I owed the First National Bank of Birmingham $650,000. In 1930, business was so bad, I went to see Metropolitan and asked them to take the building. I thank God they did not take it. I made arrangements to pay them $3,000 a month. At this time Mr. Oscar Wells, of the First National Bank, was calling me about every ten days and giving me the third degree. I offered him my business twice, but he did not take it and let me alone.*

Even though many businessmen might have seriously considered jumping out of one of the store's upper windows, Louis realized that he was fortunate to owe more than $2 million when so many people could not even borrow ten bucks. Even before the Depression hit, he had established a tradition of serving a free Thanksgiving dinner to Birmingham's needy citizens, and when the holiday season of 1929 came around, he saw no reason to let his own troubles stand in the way. One thing was certain, and that was that more people than ever would be taking part in the ritual.

The *Birmingham Age-Herald* reported, "There will be no hungry people in Birmingham on Thanksgiving Day if Louis Pizitz can prevent it. Following an annual custom, invitations have been extended to every deserving, needy person in the city, both white and Negro, to share in a free, bountiful dinner provided at the Pizitz Store from 12 to 2 p.m. on Thursday." The article went on to specify that no dinners were to be taken away from the store; they had to be consumed on the premises.

Apparently, even with so many people in destitute conditions, there were certain Birmingham citizens who tried to maintain what they thought was an attitude of superiority. When Thanksgiving 1930 arrived and the Depression had not gotten any better, the *Age-Herald* mentioned a change to the "no take-out" policy of the previous year: "The meal will be cooked in the Pizitz kitchen and served in the basement store. Seats and tables will be placed to accommodate 400 people at one time. Negroes will be given their dinners on a covered plate to be taken home." Yes, things weren't so rosy for everyone, but most of the participants just seemed happy to eat, whether or not they were allowed to do so on the premises. The Pizitz employees, who technically were given the day off from work, reported for duty regardless and took up their positions in the makeshift dinner hall to serve the feast.

By 1932, even Louis Pizitz must have been wondering if the country would ever pull out of its financial tailspin, and much of the public had reason for doubt as well. That year's article reported that the waiting line consisted of "old people who have lost hope in life; young people wondering if hope will ever return; a young woman with her baby in her arms; whole families waiting together in line." The reporter noted that there was a somber mood about the crowd, as many of the people present had never before had to take advantage of a free dinner. Again crossing any religious barriers as if they never existed, Louis had enlisted the help of his friend, Birmingham's beloved pastor Brother Bryan, to ask the blessing.

The needs of the suffering were most obvious during the Thanksgiving and Christmas seasons, but of course the Depression did not confine its effects to holidays. Louis later recalled an event when he really stuck his own neck out, even as it looked like the blade of a guillotine was ready to fall on it:

In 1930, the State of Alabama could not pay its schoolteachers and had to give them scrip. This scrip sold for 75 cents in merchandise at first and finally got down to 50 cents on the dollar in merchandise. I had about $75,000 worth of this scrip, and in 1931 the First National Bank, which was about running the store as I had to put up my stock for loans, told me not to take any more scrip as it would never be paid out. My son-in-law told me not to take any more, for the bank would find it out and take away our business from us. I took it anyway and put it in my pocket, then turned it over to my wife to keep. All together, I had $178,000 in teachers' scrip, and in 1934 the state borrowed eighteen million dollars and paid these off one hundred cents to the dollar. I sold some of mine for 102, and this is when I started coming back in business.

Even with all of this turmoil, Louis somehow found the money in 1931 to build his own estate on Shades Mountain. Named Happydale, the imposing home sat on five hundred acres in what would later become the city of Vestavia Hills.

No matter how difficult Louis found his own financial affairs, he continued to put up an optimistic face for the people of his adopted home city. In July 1932, the *Birmingham News* ran an article that amounted to a two-column editorial by the Pizitz store's magnate, whom it stated had just returned from a business trip to the East Coast. Louis's keen interest in world affairs was demonstrated by his cautionary remarks about the United States' role in the war that seemed to be brewing overseas. "Unless conditions in Europe, particularly in England, Germany, Italy and France, are on a satisfactory, settled basis, we as a nation are bound to suffer through their suffering," he said.

Closer to home, he saw great promise in the nomination of Franklin D. Roosevelt for president at the summer political conventions and predicted that when a proposed $2 billion relief bill was passed, things would begin looking rosier for Birmingham because the city "is sure to get a tremendous amount of orders for pipe, cement and the other materials necessary for construction work done in the South."

Despite the continuing effects of the Depression, Pizitz kept making merry whenever the Christmas season approached. Beginning in the late 1920s and continuing through the Depression years, the store sponsored a three-days-a-week Santa Claus program over radio station WBRC. Children were encouraged to send in "Santagrams" to the jolly old elf, who would then read them over the air and offer "promises and suggestions" to the

Santa Claus

Talks To The Children

WBRC 7:15 p. m.

MONDAY — WEDNESDAY — FRIDAY

From his headquarters at Pizitz he will read the Santagrams which children send him.

P I Z I T Z

Pizitz sponsored a thrice-weekly visit with Santa Claus over radio station WBRC. Children who sent "Santagrams" to the jolly old elf would get a personal response from him and might even hear their letter read over the air. *Birmingham Public Library collection.*

listeners. Those who sent in such communiqués would receive in return a seemingly handwritten letter on a green-and-red letterhead from "Pizitz & Santa Claus, Dispensers of Happiness." The letter, which sounds rather like it might have been crafted by Louis himself, read:

> *I sure was glad to get your Santagram. It was nice and very helpful to me to have you write me what you want. Your parents say you are trying very hard to be good. That's what I like—I love good little boys and girls. When I come down the chimney on Christmas, I hope I can bring all the things you want. Your old friend, Santa Claus.*

Even jolly old St. Nick could not have prevented a near tragedy that occurred in Pizitz's neighborhood. On March 10, 1934, a fire that began in the Loveman's subbasement infiltrated the aging store's brick walls and oil-soaked wooden floors, turning the entire landmark structure into an inferno. The Pizitz building a block south was not in harm's way, although there was plenty of smoke damage in the former Louis Saks store that stood between the two. By this time, it had become known as Melancon's department store, and the story was later told how the store's telephone operator remained at her switchboard, choking on smoke, until she could place a long-distance call to the traveling Clem Melancon and secure his official permission to close.

This unusual angle demonstrates the positions of Pizitz, competitor Loveman's (at far right, the new 1935 building after the disastrous fire) and Melancon's (later J.J. Newberry) standing between the two like a referee. The Newberry building was later demolished to make way for the McWane Science Center's Imax Theater. *Birmingham, Ala. Public Library Archives, Cat. #BN500.*

(The Melancon building was also partly leased by the J.J. Newberry five-and-ten chain. A couple of years after this brush with disaster, Clem Melancon turned over the whole building to Newberry's, which went on to become the last surviving downtown Birmingham department store.)

The role Louis Pizitz and his building played during the Loveman's fire would be recounted by eyewitnesses repeatedly for decades. Fortunately, there were no casualties among Loveman's customers that busy Saturday morning, as the staff had done a remarkable job of getting them all outside before the interior burst into flames. That left the overwhelmed Birmingham firefighters whose job it was to battle the blaze, however. The Pizitz main floor was opened as a sort of triage area for the many firefighters who were wounded or exhausted by the losing war against the conflagration. A commemorative booklet published at the time noted how Pizitz's merchandise was quickly removed so the sales counters could serve as makeshift hospital beds. An eyewitness noted that Louis Pizitz put his private automobile at the disposal of the fire department, which used it to transport victims to the hospital or to their homes. One ambulance driver related another story of Louis's willingness to help: "He supplied our ambulances with clean, dry linens and blankets. When his men begged him to leave and go home, he refused. Generously he gave innumerable pairs of gloves and shoes to the firemen. From his store he had coffee and sandwiches sent to the fighting men."

The great Loveman's fire would always remain in people's memories as one of the turning points in downtown Birmingham history. By the time a modern, Art Deco–influenced Loveman's arose on the same spot in November 1935, Pizitz would have had a chance to regain some of the footing it had lost during the worst Depression years. As Louis wrote many years later, "In 1935 I paid out to the bank about $250,000 and I paid Metropolitan Life Insurance Co. $300,000 and then I started making money again."

The dark finally turned into light on Christmas Eve 1936, when the First National Bank of Birmingham delivered "all the stock of the Louis Pizitz Dry Goods Company and Pizitz Realty Company, which you had

In 1935, representatives of Kellogg's and Kelvinator teamed up to demonstrate their products in Pizitz's seventh-floor auditorium. This photo identifies the participants as (left to right) Pizitz's M.K. Erdreich; Kellogg's demonstrator, Winifred Loggan; Kellogg's state manager, John Bradford; Kelvinator demonstrator Lucille Martin; and WBRC radio announcer Charles Wright. *Author's collection.*

lodged with us under an agreement of several years back," as the cheery letter phrased it. "The spirit of the contract has been fulfilled." On May 31, 1939, Walter E. Henley, chairman of the board of Birmingham Trust and Savings Company, sent Louis a congratulatory letter upon the observance of the store's fortieth anniversary and related the following anecdote: "I happened to be a bank teller and opened your account upon the occasion of you starting your first store. I have in mind what that deposit was and it was no more than the sales of your present store would be in a few minutes. So, in testifying to your growth and development, it is all very real to me, for I was present at the beginning." Strange, isn't it, how the same people who can hound someone for money when they are down and out can turn out to be "ol' buddy, ol' pal, ol' chum" once the same party is doing well financially?

These happy monetary events were offset by the death of Louis's wife Minnie at age sixty-five on June 13, 1937. As proven by his autobiographical

Pizitz was proud of its fleet of delivery trucks, seen lined up in front of the store in the late 1930s. By this time, if anyone was not aware that Pizitz was known as "Your Store," they must have needed a visit to the optical department. *Birmingham, Ala. Public Library Archives, Cat. #OVH1153.*

musings of years later, he never forgot that it was Minnie's dissatisfaction with rural Swainsboro that had led him to move to Birmingham in the first place. At her funeral, the honorary pallbearers were a who's who list of Birmingham retail of the era: Joseph H. Loveman, Jake Burger and Louis Phillips, Harold Blach, Clem Melancon and Robert Aland, among many other friends of the family. In an extraordinary move, the Pizitz store was closed for two days—something that even the Depression and the Loveman's fire had been unable to do.

By this time, Louis's son Isadore was becoming more and more prominent in the store's affairs. He was born on April 3, 1903, coincidentally his father's thirty-sixth birthday. Isadore spent his elementary and high school years in the Birmingham public school system. After attending Washington and Lee University and the Wharton School of Business at the University of Pennsylvania, Isadore returned to Birmingham and was appointed president of Louis Pizitz Dry Goods Company in 1924.

Louis also had two daughters: Bertha—who was older than Isadore—and Silvia, who was the youngest of the siblings. Bertha was never directly involved in any of the operations of the store, although her husband, Joseph Smolian, did make a career with the company for years. (He was no doubt the son-in-law Louis mentioned as trying to dissuade him from accepting the schoolteachers' scrip.) Silvia became a noted art collector in New York City, where she also spent many years as a buyer in the Pizitz stores' office.

One mystery concerning Isadore is the newspaper ad that ran on Saturday, March 2, 1940, urging everyone to tune in to a "message of the utmost importance to every man, woman and child living in Birmingham and Alabama." This world-shaking speech was to be delivered over radio stations WBRC (3:00 p.m.), WSGN (5:00 p.m.) and WAPI (9:45 p.m.). Seventy years later, it is impossible to know with any certainty just what Isadore was going to speak about—but considering that on Monday, March 4, the store advertised "the South's greatest sale, Pizitz $100,000 Day," Isadore's sons have to speculate that their dear old dad was giving a stump speech to encourage people to shop at Pizitz.

The occasional radio broadcast aside, newspapers were still Pizitz's primarily means of advertising, and sometimes the ads took on a colossal size and scale. The store continued to acknowledge its anniversary every April, but this would often be conflated with an annual "June Celebration" that dated back to the days before the 1925 building was constructed. A double-page ad on June 2, 1940, packed much of the Pizitz philosophy into its allotted space, beginning with yet another statement over Louis's personal signature:

The sign on the hood of this truck making a delivery to the Cambridge Apartments is advertising Pizitz's thirty-ninth anniversary, giving us a pretty good clue that the photo comes from sometime in 1938. *Birmingham, Ala. Public Library Archives, Cat. #OVH1161.*

Tomorrow I begin the celebration of my 41st business birthday. From an insignificant beginning, my store grew steadily and rapidly until it became, and has been for many years, the largest store in Alabama. [One can almost see Louis sticking his tongue out at Loveman's, which had so proudly promoted that claim in the past.]

I know to whom credit for all this belongs. I have never forgotten the customers of the early days who had confidence in me when I hadn't so much in myself. I am ever mindful of and grateful to the thousands who shop with me day in and day out, who depend on me to give them the best and the most for their money.

The same ad contained another statement under the headline "Our Business Is Storekeeping." While not signed by Louis, it is a fascinating peek at the attitude taken by his staff:

We don't play the stock market; we don't speculate in real estate. We don't have branch stores. We wouldn't become part of a chain if they gave us the chain. Our business is running this store. Thousands of Alabamians look to us to safeguard their purchasing dollar, and we can do it well only by tending strictly to our knitting.

So, it isn't a matter of life or death to us if the stock market booms or collapses; we'd like to see the Barons win, but whether they do or don't is not of most importance to us; and certainly the success or lack of success of a store in Philadelphia leaves us cold. We are, of course, interested in all things pertaining to the very complex pattern life today pursues, but only as bystanders. Our one all-absorbing interest is THE STORE.

This was also the period when Pizitz acquired a longtime employee named Dolly Dale, who would still be with the store when it closed forty-six years later. The secret to such a long career is that Dolly Dale never existed— or at least not under that name. By 1940, the newspaper ads encouraged customers who could not make it to the store in person to phone in their orders to Dolly Dale. As you might gather, Dolly Dale was the name given to Pizitz's personal shopper, regardless of who might be holding down that job. The Pizitz family no longer remembers just how this particular name was coined, only that it was meant to be identifiable in the same fashion as General Foods' equally fictitious Betty Crocker. There were many Dolly Dales through the years, of course, and so successful was the program that Loveman's got into the act with its own personal shopper, Lola Lane.

Perhaps Dolly Dale was fortunate to be a fictitious character, because the real employees had many, many rules to remember on their daily jobs. The late 1930s employee handbook ran forty-three pages, crammed with dos, don'ts and suggestions on how to push more merchandise. Workers were expected to memorize the proper way to fill out sales slips for differing situations ("Cash take-with," "Cash send," "Charge take," "Charge send," "COD transaction," "Part paid COD transaction," "Cash ticket on part paid COD transaction," "COD mail transaction," "Layaway," "Even exchange transaction," "Difference in exchange transaction," "COD even exchange," "Charge take bought by someone else" and, finally, "Cash-send gift ticket"). Pizitz obviously did not want any slow-witted folks working as clerks.

And then, there were the tubes. What tubes, you ask? It might be best to let the employee handbook answer that question:

A tube system in a store is just what the name signifies—long tubes running from stations all over the store to a central room, known as the Tube Room. Cashiers are used here who make change and otherwise properly authorize delivery of merchandise by a stamp that is placed on the Send Labels of the sales ticket. Tube cups, or carriers, are tube-shaped holders having different colored felts at each end. We use the grey felted ones for cash transactions; the red felted ones for charge transactions; and the green felted ones for all C.O.D. transactions. The red carriers are also used for money orders and blank checks.

With all this to memorize, the employees hired in 1938 were probably just getting it straight in their heads by the time the United States was plunged into World War II by the Japanese attack on Pearl Harbor on December 7, 1941. While the entire country geared up for the war, Louis decided to do his part in his own unique way: he made a standing offer of $1,000 to the first man to bomb Japan.

This turned out to be no mere grandstanding move on Louis's part. General Jimmy Doolittle accepted the $1,000 gift after leading an air raid on Tokyo. Since he was unable to identify which man in his group was actually the first to drop a bomb, Doolittle endorsed the check over to the Army Air Forces Aid Society Trust Fund. The money was to be used for the widows and children of aviators who lost their lives in the ongoing battles in the Pacific.

It probably goes without saying that Louis's Polish heritage gave him a keen interest in the defeat of Hitler and his goose-stepping goons. During the height of the war in June 1943, Louis was approached to assist financially in the eventual rebuilding of Palestine, and while he was willing to help, he also used the occasion to set down on paper some of his views on being in his particular position. This letter was apparently considered so important that an original copy of it was preserved in the store's files, and numerous copies were made to be circulated about. The words Louis chose were undeniably powerful, as he wrote:

> *There is one thing I want to impress upon you…I am an American first and then a Jew. We have the greatest country in the world and we must make up our minds to do everything we can for this country regardless of religion or anything else, to show that Jews are as big American citizens as gentiles, or maybe better. I believe that out of 130 million people in our country, there are only four to five million Jews, and I feel like when you go to somebody's house you should try to behave better than in your own home. That is how I feel about this country.*
>
> *I believe the Jews ought to be better citizens than gentiles, and this has been my greatest aim in my life. If you investigate, you will find that I have always done this and am doing this now. I have been very liberal in contributing to Jewish institutions, but have given ten times as much to gentile institutions because I am living in their home.*

Louis Pizitz no doubt breathed as much of a sigh of relief as his fellow countrymen—Jewish or not—at the end of fighting in 1945. Although no

Once the United States entered World War II, Louis Pizitz became a tremendous booster for the war effort, both personally and through his store. This August 1942 window promotes a war bond rally at Legion Field, where patriotic participants could get "Victory Bucks" for each war bond they purchased and then use the makeshift money to bid on Pizitz merchandise. *Birmingham, Ala. Public Library Archives, Cat. #OVH908.*

one could have predicted it, the immediate postwar years would transform the world in which Americans lived. If those who had made it through the Roaring Twenties, the Great Depression and the war years thought they had already seen it all—well, they had several decades of surprises in store for them in just the next fifteen years, and the Pizitz store would be right there to deliver each and every one of them.

Chapter 3

GOING UP

O nce all the fighting was over, it did not take the United States long
to readjust to peacetime. The biggest adjustment was that the new
postwar world was hardly anything like the world before 1941. Probably due
to the heightened tempo of things during the conflict, life in 1946 somehow
seemed faster-paced, slicker and, with the boom of postwar prosperity, ready
for new things almost every month.

In this new world, the Pizitz store gradually ceased being a personal
extension of Louis Pizitz, as it had been up to that point. Louis was still
around but was in his late seventies and was leaving much of the daily
business to son Isadore. He still appeared for major functions and events, but
no longer did every newspaper ad carry his signature, nor did every article
feel it necessary to recount his many philanthropic efforts of the past. Maybe
that was another feature of the new postwar world—people were ready to
forget the "old days" and move on with the promise of tomorrow.

By 1946, Pizitz was the official source for textbooks used in the Birmingham
and Jefferson County school systems. The store had been doing a booming
book business for quite some time; in fact, for a while it even had its own
lending library. The relationship between Pizitz and the schools must have
been a chummy one indeed, because even the holders for the Jefferson
County report cards were imprinted with the store logo.

Another relationship that continued was Pizitz's kinship with WBRC radio.
In 1946, the station was still broadcasting the seasonal Santa Claus program;
that year, St. Nicholas arrived in Pizitz's second-floor toy department on

In November 1946, Pizitz teamed up with radio station WAPI to install an electric news sign on the corner of the store building, in the fashion of the famous crawling signage of Times Square. The sign lasted for only a couple of years at the most. *Birmingham Public Library collection.*

the first Saturday of November, betraying those folks of today who claim that "back when I was a kid" the Christmas season did not begin until after Thanksgiving. Being that Pizitz and WBRC were such old friends, the move the store made at the end of that month seems a bit odd.

Through newsreels and photographs, the general public had been made aware of the huge electric news sign in New York's Times Square, which ran a continual crawl of headlines throughout the day and night. Pizitz made arrangements not with WBRC but with competing station WAPI to install a similar (though smaller) electric news sign on its Second Avenue/Nineteenth Street corner. The sign was placed between the second- and third-floor windows, just above the neon letters that still proclaimed Pizitz as "Your Store." The newspaper explained just how such a sign worked in those pre-computerized days:

From early in the morning until late at night, news taken from WAPI's wire service is flashed over the sign. The news "tape" is punched in the WAPI studios and placed in a Trans-Lux transmitter, which sends the coded signals instantly over leased telegraph wires to Pizitz. News on the sign will be kept "live," since splicing "flashes" into the tape requires only 90 seconds, or about the same time as it would take an announcer to reach a microphone.

Just how long Pizitz and WAPI kept up their running news headlines is not clear. It is true that most people do not remember the electric sign, and it shows up in very few photos of the building, so its tenure could not have been very long. Likely the arrival of television in Birmingham during the summer of 1949 would have rendered it obsolete if it even lasted that long.

More lasting changes were taking place inside the store. During the summer of 1947, a "million dollar improvement program" was implemented, and the first completed step in the multipart procedure was certainly a welcome one for summer shoppers: for the first time, all floors of the store were air conditioned. Even with that, well into the 1950s Pizitz joined with the other downtown stores in a tradition of closing all day on Wednesdays during July and August to give the employees and shoppers a break from the heat.

The rest of the time, customers needed a better way to travel from one air-cooled floor to another, so just in time for the Christmas season, another innovation was unveiled on November 24, 1947. Now folks could ride the "moving stairways," aka escalators, from the street level up to the fourth floor. (Any higher than that required the use of the old-fashioned elevators.) These new escalators were an obvious point of pride for Pizitz. When Loveman's had been rebuilt after the 1934 fire, Birmingham's first escalator had been put into service between that store's first and second floors. Pizitz pooh-poohed that notion by extending its escalator service to what amounted to Loveman's entire four-story structure. (Loveman's would follow in 1955, and Pizitz would finally get escalators to the fifth and sixth floors in the mid-1960s.)

The opening of the new Pizitz escalators was treated as if it were a major event. Besides Louis and Isadore, also taking part were Birmingham mayor Cooper Green, officials of Westinghouse—the manufacturer of the escalators—and actress Mary "Bebe" Anderson, billed as "Birmingham's gift to Hollywood and Broadway," who untied a red bow to start the escalators' motion. (Anderson's list of movie and television credits is a long and impressive one, but her most famous role was as Maybelle Merriwether in *Gone with the Wind*.) Isadore made a short speech, but as usual, Louis

Nothing had prepared the public for such a sight as the Pizitz escalator system dedicated in November 1947. While it was true that Loveman's had an earlier escalator between the first and second floors, Pizitz beat its rival to the punch with "moving stairways" all the way up to the fourth floor. *Author's collection.*

chimed in with his now traditional recounting of his feelings: "I came to Birmingham 49 years ago and opened a small store on this corner. [The order and dates of those historical events had obviously been changed once again.] I worked very hard—I still do—and I never lost confidence in myself or Birmingham. I knew Birmingham would be a great city, and I knew my store would someday be a big store in that great city."

The escalators were said to have a capacity of forty thousand people per hour, or the equivalent of ten additional elevators. The moving stairway system even became the star of its own Pizitz radio show, as WAPI's Maury Farrell filled up airtime on Tuesday and Thursday mornings by riding the escalators with his mobile microphone and interviewing shoppers. The show's title? What else—*Going Up*.

The escalators were the opening act for one of Pizitz's biggest promotional pushes in 1948: the unveiling of the "new fashion floor." The days when Pizitz was known as the store for poor people and Loveman's was for the upper class had been disintegrated by the postwar prosperity boom, and the revamping of the women's department on the third floor was a sure sign that Pizitz was heading in a new direction.

There was the unusual step of having the store keep its regular 10:00 a.m. to 5:30 p.m. hours, but for the grand opening of the fashion floor, the store reopened from 7:00 to 9:00 p.m. so shoppers could inspect the new facility and enjoy the music of the DeWitt Shaw Orchestra. Strolling models known as the Lorraine Girls showed off the last fashions, while there were radio broadcasts at regular intervals on WBRC, WAPI, WSGN, WTNB and WAFM. (The WTNB broadcast at 8:30 p.m. was particularly notable because it was co-hosted by Evelyn Allen, who would go on to direct the broadcast advertising for rival store Parisian in future years.)

Pizitz's design for the third floor also showed that the lean years were over. The ads crowed over the ten separate areas, each of which played its own role in trend setting: the Sumptuous Crown Room ("apparel from foremost designers presented in the most luxurious setting"), the Bridal Salon, the Shoe Salon with its turquoise walls, the Millinery Salon, the Junior Shops,

"...Eh, Doc!

I'll be at Pizitz this

Saturday morning at 11"

WITH FREE LOLLIPOPS FOR ALL MY LITTLE FRIENDS

* HE WALKS...HE TALKS...HE'S 7 FEET TALL
* HE ARRIVES FROM NORTH BUNNYVILLE VIA SOUTHERN AIRWAYS 9:30 SATURDAY MORNING
* GO OUT TO THE AIRPORT AND SEE HIM LAND
* THERE'LL BE MUSIC BY BILL NAPPI'S BAND
* THERE'LL BE A PARADE DOWNTOWN TO PIZITZ

It's Mr. Bunny
in person

Mr. Bunny will make
Pizitz Bunnyland his
headquarters from
Saturday until Easter

HAVE YOUR CHILD'S PHOTO
TAKEN WITH MR. BUNNY
1.00

BUY THE KIDS A HELIUM
FILLED EASTER BALLOON
15c

Pizitz
1899 GOLDEN YEAR 1949

From the 1940s to the 1970s, the annual arrival of the Easter Bunny was almost as big a deal for Pizitz as Santa Claus comin' to town. In 1949, the holiday rodent bore an uncanny resemblance to a certain wascally wabbit of Warner Bros. cartoon fame. *Author's collection.*

the Fur Salon (with more than $250,000 in furs), the Sportswear Shop, the Dress Shops, the Suit-Coat Shops and, finally, forty-five spacious fitting rooms. And remember, folks—these were the improvements in only a single floor of the seven-story building.

By this time, Easter had developed into almost as important a promotional season for Pizitz as Christmas. A Pizitz Easter egg hunt at Avondale Park was instituted in 1947 and held each year well into the 1960s. In those pre-TV days, the annual search for colored henfruit was heavily promoted through the weekly meetings of the Mickey Mouse Club at the Alabama Theatre, with additional assistance from WBRC radio. Never willing to let a sales opportunity pass by, the ads also stated that extra prizes would be available to those kiddies who happened to be wearing clothes purchased on Pizitz's second floor.

Also found on the second floor was the Easter Bunny in "person," or whatever one might call a seven-foot-tall rabbit. His annual arrival was the subject of newspaper headlines, and once the big bunny hopped into town each year, he would be ensconced in Pizitz's second-floor "Bunnyland." Unfortunately, no photos or even newspaper descriptions exist to tell us just what Bunnyland was or what kids could see there, but if they had gotten up enough courage to sit on Santa's lap four months before, they could reasonably be expected to consort with the giant jackrabbit with a minimum of trauma.

No sooner had January 2, 1949, arrived than the Birmingham newspapers were inundated with the first wave of Pizitz's yearlong fiftieth-anniversary

Nothing less than Pizitz's fiftieth-anniversary celebration in 1949 could have caused the huge "Your Store" neon letters to be taken down and replaced with a different slogan. *Birmingham, Ala. Public Library Archives, Cat. #820.11.28.*

celebration. This massive sales pitch even caused the traditional "Your Store" signage on the Nineteenth Street and Second Avenue sides of the building to be replaced with new neon letters spelling out "Golden Year." (Photos from this period also show definitely that the electric news sign was no longer in place.) That was also the year that television finally came to Birmingham, with WAFM (Channel 13) and WBRC (Channel 4, later Channel 6) coming on the air within days of each other. Pizitz wasted no time moving into the new realm of TV advertising. Its big program was a Monday night game of charades on Channel 13.

If you think charades is an odd choice for television entertainment, you are obviously unaware that in those primitive days, Channel 13 would routinely fill fifteen minutes or a half hour of the broadcast day by showing a record playing on a turntable. Sometimes, if a director were feeling especially creative, some windup toys from Woolworth's or Kress would be placed on the table to hop around while the music played. So, don't laugh—the *Pizitz Charades* show was a big deal. A box was placed next to the street-floor escalator for shoppers to drop in their suggestions for on-air charades… audience participation at its most basic.

Many people were totally unprepared for the power of television. The medium made white-hot superstars out of performers who had been considered footnotes in show business up to that point. Take the case of

Pizitz's display designers were responsible for keeping all twenty-two display windows updated on a weekly basis. Sometimes they were elaborate works of art, but at other times they were more utilitarian, as with this line of Tom Cat jeans for less than two bucks. *Author's collection.*

screen cowboy William Boyd, aka Hopalong Cassidy. His B-Western movies had been popular draws in theaters since the 1930s, but he was hardly considered a star of the Clark Gable variety. Once his old films began running on local television stations, though, what had been a steady popularity blazed into an all-out craze. That is where things stood when Pizitz brought Boyd/Hopalong to Birmingham for a personal appearance in September 1951.

The next day, the newspapers reported on the all-out pandemonium that engulfed Pizitz on this occasion. The final count was that approximately thirty thousand people—that's not *three* thousand, but *thirty* thousand, ladies and gentlemen—jammed the department store for the opportunity to glimpse the black-suited, silver-haired cowpoke. The reason the numbers had to be estimated is that Pizitz had set up an automatic counting machine, but after an hour and a half it was destroyed by the crush of people, having counted fifteen thousand up to that point. The reporter noted, "The jovial Mr. Hopalong took the crowds in stride, shaking hands with hundreds, smiled a beaming movie-star smile and noticed practically every one of his idolizers." The writer also marveled, as well he should, over the fact that Boyd had a policy of never charging a public appearance fee.

A few years later, a similar scene would be repeated with a Pizitz visit by an even larger national phenomenon: Fess Parker, whom Walt Disney had picked from relative obscurity and turned into the living embodiment of Davy Crockett. Parker made his visit to Pizitz at the end of May 1955, not quite six months after his first Crockett stories had aired on Disney's Wednesday night television program. This time, even though Isadore Pizitz was photographed with Parker and acknowledged as sponsor of the visit, the newspapers paid much more attention to the hysteria that greeted buckskin-bundled Parker from the moment his plane touched down at the Birmingham airport.

Whereas Hopalong had battled the crowds at Pizitz and then got out of Dodge, Fess Parker was greeted by thousands of kids and their families lining the streets from the airport all the way downtown, waiting to wave to Parker in his motorcade. He was presented with the key to the city, did an interview for WABT-TV (on which the weekly Disney show was seen) and then was whisked to the Tutwiler Hotel for a press breakfast the next morning before hanging out at Pizitz for a while and then visiting the shut-in youngsters at the Crippled Children's Hospital and Hillman Hospital. Pizitz might not have made the news as much as the store might have liked, but there was no doubt that it had been responsible for bringing coonskin-capped Crockett to town.

Just as stores today have departments devoted to Barbie or Disney characters, in August 1950 Pizitz built an entire area devoted to that straight-shootin' cowboy Hopalong Cassidy. The merchandise was a big enough hit but was nothing compared to the pandemonium when the star visited the little buckaroos in person in September 1951. *Author's collection.*

(In all the excitement, seemingly no one thought to call attention to the fact that the *real* Davy Crockett had spent some time in Jones Valley, future site of Birmingham, during some of his pioneering expeditions in 1818. Obviously not as many people turned out to see the real thing as his latter-day television counterpart.)

The crazy 1950s had barely gotten started when Pizitz made its first major expansion since the two-part construction of its flagship building.

In February 1952, Pizitz opened its new Store for Men in what had formerly been the neighboring Goold Shop. The advertising and display departments were located in the upper floors of this annex building. *Dixie Neon collection.*

Louis Pizitz, still holding his own as chairman of the board, announced that the Goold Shop, a three-story clothing store that adjoined Pizitz on the Second Avenue side—separating Pizitz from the Aland family's New Ideal store—had been acquired for "several hundred thousand dollars." The December 31, 1950 revelation of this purchase stated that the new space, which Louis compared to an entire additional floor in square footage, would be known as the Pizitz Goold Annex.

There must have been a change in plans during the year it took to convert the Goold Shop, because when the grand reopening was held on February 8, 1952, there were no references to Goold to be found, and the new signage proudly proclaimed the new addition as Pizitz Store for Men. The newspaper coverage mentioned that the new Store for Men "will carry a complete line of men's clothing, sportswear, shoes and luggage." In this way, it sounds much like a lower-key answer to the lavish women's fashion floor that had gotten so much earlier publicity. Shoppers could enter the Store for Men through either a sidewalk entrance or from the main floor of the regular Pizitz building. The upper two floors of the annex, as it was known to Pizitz employees, became the home to the advertising and display departments.

One of the employees who came to work for Pizitz during this period was Lena Brigman. It is fortunate for future historians that in October 2000, a couple of years after Lena's death, her daughter Allene saw fit to set down

Even years after the escalators were first put into service, they often served as a backdrop for special events, such as this appearance by what seems to be a Salvation Army worker during the Christmas season. *Birmingham Public Library collection.*

on paper some memories of her mother's time with Pizitz. These seemingly random thoughts somehow mesh together to give a most evocative portrait of a large department store in the 1950s:

> *My mom went to work at Pizitz in 1953, at first part time and shortly after, full time in the basement linen department. At the time, I believe the linen department was down the steps from the 19ᵗʰ Street entrance, but later moved to back next to the pharmacy. Mom took so much pride in her work. She kept the department so tidy. She could fold a fitted sheet like nobody else could. Mom loved Pizitz and all the people who worked there. She thought of them as family.*
>
> *I remember the big sales, the Dollar Days and the $100,000 Dollar Days. Sometimes merchandise would be advertised that wasn't available, and customers sometimes got very mad. Mom was so calm and would*

Catalogues were a year-round sales outlet for Pizitz. This spring 1954 notions catalogue featured everything from cedar wardrobes to bedroom slippers, and, of course, we cannot ignore the voluminous skirt modeled by the lady on the front cover. *Author's collection.*

try to explain about the merchandise. Once she received a note from her boss, David Sharp, telling about a customer in North Carolina who called long distance for the sole purpose of complimenting Mom on her outstanding service.

My own best memories of Pizitz were running down the steps to the basement to see my sweet, smiling Mama. I remember all the toys, the beautiful animated windows filled with snow at Christmas, and the music piped through the store. I remember the Hole in the Wall food bar with its delicious barbecue sandwiches for 29 cents. I remember Mom working late, sometimes on Monday nights and sometimes on Friday nights, at Christmas time. We would come early to pick her up so we could stay in the store and visit all her friends. My son was little and he loved the toy department.

There was nothing like shopping in downtown Birmingham when Pizitz and Loveman's and Newberry's were there. It was safe and fun. How great it would be to have the good old days back.

As the largest store in the state, and with the crowds that flocked downtown every Christmas season, it was no exaggeration for Pizitz to call itself "Alabama's Santa Claus." *Author's collection.*

Downtown in general, and Pizitz in particular, might have been special places—but the downtown Pizitz store was not the only Pizitz. There had been a Pizitz store in Bessemer dating all the way back to 1926. But, wait… remember that in 1940, the forty-first-anniversary ad had unequivocally stated that Pizitz had no branch stores? That was true, so how could this situation exist? The Pizitz family explains that the original Bessemer store was founded by Levi Becker, a relative of the family. Through some arrangement with Louis Pizitz, he was allowed to use the name for his store even though it otherwise had no connection with the downtown institution. This was before the era of franchising caught on, so the arrangement must have been a rather informal one among kinfolk.

In 1956, there was a pile of publicity surrounding the fact that an all-new, modern Bessemer Pizitz was to be built, and this time it was really and truly going to be the first branch store, with Isadore's oldest son, Richard, as president. Levi Becker and his son Jack were to remain as operating heads of the new store, which was to be built on the site of the original: 1915–21 Second Avenue North in Bessemer. The fact that both the downtown and Bessemer stores occupied space near Nineteenth Street and Second Avenue North in their respective cities was surely a mere coincidence.

(While on the subject of the Pizitz branch stores, it might be worth mentioning here that there was also a Pizitz in Tuscaloosa. This, however, was an enterprise begun by a completely different side of the family. Max Pizitz had emigrated from Poland in 1911 and began Tuscaloosa's Pizitz Mercantile Company in 1913. It later passed into the hands of his sons, Sam and Isadore—yes, a different Isadore Pizitz than Louis's son who ran the Birmingham stores. After opening stores downtown, in MacFarland Mall and in Alberta City, Pizitz of Tuscaloosa went out of business in 1981, and no doubt confused and confounded many commuters between Tuscaloosa and Birmingham during the nearly seventy years it was in operation.)

Meanwhile, back in Bessemer, no effort was spared to make the new store a showplace. With a whole new building, not a 1920s structure, the Pizitz family was free to literally build from the ground up. A newspaper article gasped, "The new store will be completely air-conditioned, offering the newest type elevator service. The store will have acoustical ceilings and vinyl floor covering. The store front will feature porcelain enamel, aluminum setting bars and plate glass windows with brick trim, and channel-type sign with neon lighting in back."

NEW PIZITZ STORE TO BE BUILT IN BESSEMER
. . . Construction will start shortly on development

When the announcement came out in 1956 that Pizitz was going to open its first branch store in Bessemer, the news was treated as a major retail event. *Birmingham Public Library collection.*

44

The all-new Bessemer Pizitz had its formal grand opening on September 17, 1956, when the ceremonial ribbon was cut by Louis Pizitz and Jack Becker's three-year-old daughter, Fran. Richard Pizitz handled master of ceremonies chores. All the hoopla was as if Bessemer had never had a Pizitz store before, especially when Mayor Jess Lanier boomed, "We welcome you with all our heart." Indeed, Bessemer had had a Pizitz store, but not a store owned by the Pizitzes. Is it making any sense now?

Perhaps seeing all the modern new facilities in Bessemer made the family do some heavy thinking regarding the flagship downtown store. During the sixtieth-anniversary celebration in April

This full-page newspaper ad from April 15, 1959, kicked off Pizitz's sixtieth-anniversary celebration. The designers had to use their imagination to depict the first Pizitz store, since no photos of it were, or are, known to exist. *Author's collection.*

1959, Isadore announced the commencement of a $1 million remodeling program that would transform every floor of the old building. On the main street floor, "not a single fixture now in use will remain," the press release boasted. All of the other floors were to receive a face-lift, with the seventh floor becoming a seven-hundred-seat auditorium made available to clubs and civic organizations.

It is significant that Louis Pizitz was absent from any of the announcements about the latest modernization program. Turning ninety-two years old the same month his store turned sixty, Louis was in failing health but continued to remain in his business for as long as possible. He had a beautiful wood-

This page: On Christmas Eve 1958, Louis and Isadore Pizitz participated in the annual bestowing of gifts upon their employees. It would be Louis's final time to do this, as he passed away six months later. *Pizitz family collection.*

paneled office on the fifth floor, but he much preferred to hang around the lady customers on the fashionable third floor, where he sat in an easy chair and hobnobbed with the crowds for hours. He continually referred to the employees as "my children," and most of them felt the same affection for him.

We have seen repeatedly that some parts of Pizitz's history are now cloudy because there was no real attempt to archive or document the story as it was unfolding. Sometimes historical pieces seem to have been preserved strictly by accident. One of those pieces is an anonymous article that ran in the Albertville, Alabama newspaper during the late 1950s. Although the writer purposely did not identify Louis Pizitz by name, the fact that someone thought to file it away is a sure indicator that everyone knew whom it concerned. The writer said:

> *The rain was peppering down as I approached the building in the big city, and I noticed a chauffeur employing both arms and hands in assisting his aged employer to the entrance. He wore a heavy coat and pulled-down hat as a protection against the weather, and I couldn't see his face. The big doors to the foyer were closed, and I hurried to reach them first and hold them open to simplify their entrance.*
>
> *It was surprising that one so apparently ill would even notice, but he stopped and asked, "What is your name? I should like to shake hands with you." It was only then that I recognized him as a great philanthropist, about whom I have often read.*
>
> *"Oh, you are Mr. _____, aren't you?" "Yes," he replied, "but how did you know?" "I have seen you many times and your pictures often," I explained. He then clasped my hand and entered the elevator.*
>
> *When a feeble and violently ill person can make the effort to express gratitude for such a small courtesy, it surely behooves all of us to be considerate.*

Since Louis's debilitated condition was obvious to all, even when he was not identified by name, it probably should have come as no surprise when the *Birmingham News* headlines blared the news of his death early in the day of June 22, 1959. The obituary article dutifully repeated the same litany of stories of his philanthropy that had been related for years: his Thanksgiving Day dinners for the poor, his trips to the city and county jails in company with Brother Bryan to deliver Christmas feasts, his buying of the coal mines to put the workers back on the job, his accepting the schoolteachers' scrip in lieu of money and so on. "His name was spoken with affection, respect and devotion throughout the South," the newspaper writer surmised. An editorial the next day put it in more detailed terms:

> One thinks of Louis Pizitz warmly and with deep regret at his death. He was warm, a gentle soul, and possessed a sure sense of humor mixed with much wisdom as to the ways of life. One story of him gently displays this. It is said—and we do not know whether it is accurate or apocryphal—that he once encountered a woman shopper during his roaming about his store. She inquired as to whether some item was a bargain. His soft reply was said to be that nothing was a bargain if you did not need it. His death will leave us with a great emptiness. He was in and of the spirit of Birmingham.

Perhaps the greatest indication of the esteem in which Louis was held was not the glowing newspaper accounts of his life but the plethora of ads

Tomorrow morning Thursday, July 2, 1959, Main floor 9:30 A.M. A special Memorial Program honoring Mr. Louis Pizitz

You are cordially invited to attend a special Memorial Program honoring our beloved founder, "Big Pop".

We feel that this will be an experience which you will always cherish.

This printed flyer with Louis Pizitz's familiar face invited all employees to a special memorial service for their late patriarch a couple of weeks after his death on June 22, 1959. *Author's collection.*

that were taken out by the other downtown stores in order to pay tribute to him during the following days. Some, such as Yeilding's and Burger-Phillips, used their ad space for simple acknowledgement, but others went further. Loveman's knew it was time to temporarily set aside the traditional rivalry and stated, "Our deepest sympathy to the family, associates and many friends of Mr. Louis Pizitz. We mourn his passing, and salute his important personal contributions to the business life and welfare agencies of Birmingham." The New Ideal, still adjoining the Pizitz Store for Men, enumerated Louis's accomplishments as "a close friend, wonderful neighbor, outstanding citizen, leading philanthropist, and great humanitarian."

The most elaborate eulogy from a competitor was placed in an ad by Sears, Roebuck and Company:

> *Louis Pizitz was more than a merchant, his life's work more than a great store. He was a good citizen. His deeds, his hopes, his goals—indeed, his very life personified the spirit of this town he helped to develop. Louis Pizitz was, and always will continue to be a very vital part of the spirit of the city of Birmingham and the state of Alabama. His shadow stretches far. His strength of character has supported many. His generosity was never failing. His love for his fellow man was unselfishly given. Certainly, his life was a life of honor. All who knew Louis Pizitz were fortunate. Their lives were made fuller by the experience.*

Chapter 4

CHANGING STYLES FOR CHANGING TIMES

As if anyone hadn't already figured it out from current events, Louis Pizitz's will made it crystal clear that the store's future would be controlled by Isadore, his only son, and Isadore's three sons, Richard, Michael and Merritt. Less than three months after Louis's death, this team announced its intent to build the third store in the chain. The Pizitz at Roebuck Plaza, adjacent to U.S. Highway 11 (the main route from Birmingham toward Gadsden and Chattanooga), would be the first to be situated within a shopping center rather than in a downtown locale. Even though the two-story store would be in Roebuck Plaza, it would not actually be *part* of the complex; "Land has been purchased for the new store from the Roebuck Plaza, and we will construct our own building," Isadore told the press.

He also elaborated on why the family had chosen to build its third store in that particular area. Apparently there had been a recent survey by the Harland Bartholomew city planning organization, along with an independent survey commissioned by Pizitz, and the two had given the same general answer: during the ensuing twenty years, Birmingham's primary growth was going to occur in the eastern and southern areas of the city. Initial articles said that the Pizitz in Roebuck was shooting for a July or August 1960 opening, but it turned out to be March 1961 before it was ready to welcome eastern area shoppers.

The face of retail was changing, and Pizitz's entrance into the shopping center world was but one early liver spot in the long aging process traditional shopping was about to undergo. For the present, though, things were still

At the death of his father, Isadore Pizitz became the leader of the family business. He would continue to be involved in daily operations until a week before his own death in 1985. *Author's collection.*

booming downtown. This was also the period most people remember so fondly when they think of the elaborate Christmas windows for which department stores were so famous. In Pizitz's case, these were the responsibility of display director Joe Dultz, who had come to Birmingham after a career with Bloomingdale's in New York. Each year the Pizitz windows and the other decorations carried out a different theme. For example, the ads for Christmas 1959 described that year's look: "The whole store sparkles… Pink and silver reindeer prance in a fairyland of twinkling lights on the Street Floor…every floor gleams and glitters like a giant Christmas package, filled with delightful gifts to give or to get."

Somewhat prophetically, the animated window at the corner of Second Avenue and Nineteenth Street had a "Christmas in the Forest" motif for 1959. "The animals slide and skate, dance and sing merrily around a lighted tree while preparing their Christmas feast," read the ads. During the week following Thanksgiving, sidewalk shoppers got an extra show when a small electric motor powering one of the figures became overheated and the scene burst into flames. "Spectators said the mechanical animals continued to play musical instruments and dance as the window filled with smoke," the newspaper reported the next day. "Scores of persons gathered and watched the musical dance continue even after the sprinkler system went off."

That "million dollar" remodeling program that had been announced just before Louis's death began to become evident in April 1960 when the first portion of it was unveiled: the complete overhaul of the main floor.

Although other renovations would take place during the next twenty-five years, surviving photos show that it was the 1960 project that gave the street floor what would serve as its basic look for the rest of the downtown store's life. Proving that he could carry on his father's tradition in spirit as well as in name, Isadore was quoted as saying, "There has been a lot of talk of deterioration of downtown. Pizitz has faith in downtown, as it is still the heart of the city. This completely new, modern floor is an indication of our faith not alone in Birmingham, but our faith in downtown."

The newspaper stated that everything on the first floor was new, "including entrances, windows, tile floor with bronze insets in color, new lighting and fixtures and interior decorations." Not stopping there, the report was that work would immediately begin on the new "fashion floor" on the third floor (no doubt the 1948 version was beginning to look not so fashionable anymore).

Isadore maintained his father's philanthropic reputation in other ways. He subdivided the five hundred acres that surrounded the old family estate, Happydale, and sold them off for retail and residential development. When only a few parcels were left, in December 1962 he began donating some of those to the City of Vestavia Hills. By 1968, the Jefferson County school system was thinking about building a new junior high school in the neighborhood, so the Vestavia city fathers offered a thirteen-acre parcel from the Pizitz donation. Their only stipulation in doing so was that the new

Pizitz's annual Easter egg hunt at Avondale Park was still going strong in the early 1960s. Here, an unidentified store representative (far left) participates in a WBRC broadcast with *Morning Show* hosts Tom York and Pat Gray, plus a rather short Bugs Bunny. *Author's collection.*

This 1960 toy catalogue shows the earlier Pizitz "signature" logo that would soon be updated to a bolder, fresher look to appeal to a new generation of shoppers. *Author's collection.*

facility should be named Louis Pizitz Junior High. The Jefferson County Board of Education accepted the gift of the land but balked at the name, choosing instead to call it Vestavia Hills Junior High. (The reasons for the board's unwillingness to name a school after Louis Pizitz can only be speculated, but it may well have been that the stores were so well known that it would have almost been like free advertising.)

In 1970, the citizens of Vestavia voted to form their own school system, in effect seceding from Jefferson County, and once all of the pieces fell into place, a major celebration was held on May 21, 1972, officially renaming Vestavia Hills Junior High as Louis Pizitz Middle School, which it remains today. By the time of this writing, at least a couple of generations of children who have never seen a Pizitz store in their lives are at least familiar with the name because of their school and the Pizitz Drive on which it stands. As for the original Happydale residence, it now bears the address of 2070 Vestavia Park Court.

With the benefit of hindsight, we can all see that mere cosmetic changes and altruistic activities were not going to stave off Birmingham's looming civil rights battles of the early 1960s. The downtown department stores, with their traditionally segregated restrooms, drinking fountains and lunch counters, were among the first targets in the war for equality for all. (More than one historian has commented on the fact that it was ironic that segregation was such a large part of businesses owned by the often persecuted Jewish community. The store owners, regardless of their own personal feelings about the matter, were simply following the custom—and frequently the law—of their adopted cities.)

Louis Pizitz had always cultivated a close relationship with the African American community in Birmingham. Not that his facilities were any less segregated than the others—witness the 1930s Thanksgiving dinners where only whites were invited to sit down and eat—but he had won great favor by extending his philanthropy to African American interests at a time when many other businessmen would not. A good example of the esteem in which he was held is a speech that was given by Will McAlpin, president of the Tuggle Institute—a school established specifically for homeless African American boys—and chairman of the Negro Division of the Community Chest, as it was then known. Some of the terminology McAlpin used might seem outdated to modern sensibilities, but his point was the devotion the black community felt toward this downtown merchant:

> *No man living in this county or state has done more to help the Negro race than this individual. Ever since he has been in business, the members of my race have sought him for refuge in their struggles for existence, and he has never turned one of them down. He has always recognized our race as human beings and never let our colored skins prejudice him against us. He has said that he felt that if we had been given the opportunity and education, we would have advanced much more than we have.*
>
> *Mr. Pizitz has never failed to respond to any drive put on by any church or charitable organization. Certainly the Pizitz store was the first in Birmingham to recognize our people by providing for them attractive and clean rest rooms in his great store. Others have had to follow this man's lead and provide rest rooms for the colored men and women.*

Any department store worth its floorwalkers had a bargain basement, and Pizitz's was often advertised as if it were a separate store. At one time or another, the basement also contained a pharmacy, a grocery store, a snack bar and a shoe repair department, among other features. *Author's collection.*

If it seems strange to find an African American leader with the opinion that segregated restrooms were better than no restrooms at all—well, it is obvious that a lot has changed since then. Residual goodwill was good for only so much, though, and during the summer of 1963, Pizitz found itself with a bull's-eye painted on its back just as much as any of the other downtown stores. An economic boycott by the civil rights workers had the intended crippling effect, and soon the downtown merchants met to come up with a coordinated effort to meet the challenge. Pizitz was receiving multiple bomb threats daily, all of which turned out to be false, but this did have an understandably disrupting effect on the daily routine. Richard Pizitz says that it all came to a peak one day when the White Citizens' Council was picketing the store on the Second Avenue side, trying to preserve segregation, and Martin Luther King's troops were picketing the store on the Nineteenth Street side, pushing for integration. Police stood on the corner to keep the two demonstrations from degenerating into open warfare, and at that point everyone realized that something was going to have to be done, even if it did not please all parties involved right away.

The downtown store owners agreed that their desegregation efforts had to be done simultaneously to prevent one store from becoming a target more than the others. On a designated Monday, the "white" and "colored" signs were removed from the drinking fountains at all the stores. A couple of weeks later, on another agreed-upon Monday, the same signs were banished from the restrooms. The tricky part involved the stores' restaurants. While the variety stores such as S.H. Kress, J.J. Newberry and Woolworth's had lunch counters, Pizitz, Loveman's and Sears were the three biggies with full-service restaurants. This trio came up with a predetermined Monday to allow all customers into their restaurants, regardless of race, and two of them followed through. Which one was the fink? Hint: it was *not* the one with Birmingham ownership. Over the preceding weekend, orders came down from Sears's headquarters in Chicago that the restaurant should be dismantled, so when Monday morning arrived, there was no restaurant to integrate. As for Pizitz and Loveman's, everyone stood by expecting some type of trouble, but nothing unseemly happened, and soon life was going on at its normal pace again.

Speaking of life going on, while all the racial tension was going on in Birmingham, the fourth Pizitz branch store had opened far north in Huntsville's Parkway City shopping center. Much was made of the fact that the seventy-five-thousand-square-foot store was Pizitz's first outside Jefferson County. Isadore was quoted as saying, "It is our belief that the addition of Pizitz to Parkway City's many fine stores will make this North Alabama's largest and most complete shopping center. Huntsville, its city and county officials, and the leaders of the Army's Redstone and Marshall space agencies have generated a tremendous and progressive development." Like the Huntsville space program, that city's Pizitz would prove to be one of the most durable in the chain, hanging on even as Parkway City evolved from an open-air shopping center into a mall. It even survived a direct hit from a tornado in 1974; anecdotes relate how packages of Pizitz underwear were found, still in perfect condition, on the slopes of Monte Sano Mountain.

Back home, Birmingham was certainly glad to put 1963 behind it, and in several ways, 1964 was a year of fresh beginnings for Pizitz. Not the least of these was the unveiling of a brand-new logo, the handiwork of sales promotions director Fred Rauschenberg. The store had gone through a number of distinctive logos since its founding, beginning with the earliest ones that touted the location as "the Busy Corner." During the 1920s and 1930s, the Pizitz name was spelled out in simple block letters that somewhat resembled the neon letters on the building. Several different "script" or longhand-type logos were tried out during the late 1940s, but the one that lasted for most of the next decade was at least somewhat patterned after Louis's own signature. That, however, was deemed too out-of-date for 1964 tastes.

Rauschenberg's new logo also took the form of a signature, but in a much bolder style more adaptable to being reproduced in various color combinations. It first appeared in the newspaper ads on September 27, although for several days thereafter, both the old and new logos continued to appear together. The press release that accompanied the unveiling of the new logo showed that Pizitz must also have recently gotten a bargain on a shipment of exclamation points, as it used them so profusely:

> We wanted something different! Something new and dashing that signifies the excitement now being generated at Pizitz! A symbol, firmly rooted in the past, standing on the principles of our founder, and to provide the finest in service and merchandise available! Yet it reaches toward the future as a sign of growth. It symbolizes the look of a newly revitalized store—a store with a new spark in its bloodstream—a store with faith in Alabama—a store that means tremendous savings to the young homemaker working on a tight budget—a store with constant fashion awareness! There's excitement at Pizitz—some finished, like our fourth floor, some now under construction—some still on the drawing board! All of this is embodied in our new signature! A mark that will adorn every ad, and in time, every box and bag, every truck and tag. The store with more is doing more!

If a person had a time machine and wanted to drop in on Pizitz at a most historic moment, November 1964 just might be the time to choose—so keep that in mind, you mad scientists out there. That was the month in which the annual Enchanted Forest display made its debut on the sixth floor, thanks to the efforts of Joe Dultz and his merry crew of elves. (There will be much more to say about that project in the next chapter.) Meanwhile, Pizitz announced that the store would be spending $100,000 on a new elevator system. What was so special about that, you ask? For the first time, customers would be able to take self-service elevators instead of relying on the tried-and-true elevator operators who manually controlled each car's ascent and descent. Just to allay any fears customers might have for their favorite employees,

Today, a parking deck might not seem like such an innovation, but when Pizitz opened its deck and adjoining skywalk during the 1965 Christmas shopping season, it was treated as the beginning of a new era in downtown shopping. *Birmingham Public Library collection.*

however, Pizitz made it a point to say that "all regular elevator operators will be repositioned in the Pizitz organization," putting no one out on the street. What that also meant was that Pizitz could use this turn of events to finally give the elevator operators, Molly Daniels and Adoris Hicks—who, naturally, were African American women—positions on the sales floor that would have been nonexistent in the pre–civil rights days.

The biggest November 1964 announcement would not pay off for another year, but it was treated as an event of major significance. For several years, Pizitz had supplemented the admittedly limited amount of on-the-street parallel parking with a ground-level lot at the corner of First Avenue and Eighteenth Street, diagonally across from the main store. On November 23, 1964, Isadore Pizitz revealed that a six-deck parking garage costing at least $1 million would be built on that former lot and, when finished, would accommodate 380 automobiles at a time. This was great news not only for shoppers, who would no longer have to walk the streets for sometimes blocks after finding a parking space, but also for those who were still trying to keep downtown ahead of the suburban shopping centers as a retail center. Ferd Weil of the Downtown Action Committee went on record as saying, "I consider this just the beginning of what is to come. Inadequate parking is the worst sickness of the downtown area. Now it is beginning to get proper treatment."

Even more frenzy accompanied the parking deck's formal opening in December 1965. In the interim, it had grown from six to seven stories, and one of its wonders was the way it was connected with the main store. A "skywalk," or elevated walkway, took customers from the deck into the third floor of Pizitz, which was still serving as the fashion floor for women. In fact, the skywalk came in for its own share of newsprint praise, owing to its innovative use of colored glass panels interspersed with displays of the latest dresses. Down at ground level, the ribbon-cutting ceremony was performed by a 1966 Cadillac breaking through the ribbon, representing the present and future, followed by a 1910 Maxwell (not driven by Jack Benny), representing outdated concepts of the past. Isadore Pizitz reminded everyone that some people had claimed that Louis was "building a store too big for Birmingham" when he finished the main building in 1925, but the parking deck with the same number of levels certainly validated his vision.

Speaking of validation, that was another thing that went along with the new deck. Each person who parked in it was given a ticket that was nominally good for a rate of thirty-five cents for the first hour and twenty cents for each additional hour. If the ticket were stamped with a validation notice at one of the machines located near the elevators on each floor, the rate would drop to fifteen cents an hour—a tidy savings even if no purchases were made in the store.

The mid-1960s brought with them a new determination for Pizitz to remake its image to appeal to the growing youth culture, as well as once and for all to dismantle its long-held reputation as a cheaper-class store than Loveman's. Sharon Hamrick, who came to work at the store fresh out of college in 1964, comments that up until that time, young people thought of Pizitz as the place Grandma and Grandpa went to shop. That was about to change in a big way. Here is how Hamrick described one major turning point:

A fellow named Joe Zadner had a line of dresses he called Josette Fashions. At that time, Macy's in New York was the biggest thing going, and they introduced the mini-skirt to the Northeast. If I'm not mistaken, Pizitz was the second store in the nation to introduce the mini-skirt, which was quite a coup. Now, no one had ever seen a dress this short, especially in the South. I remember we had a fashion show at The Club, and it was quite a to-do. I was one of the models, and the people there weren't quite ready for us in our mini-skirts and go-go boots! There was quite a commotion when they saw us getting out of the limousines, but then Dick Pizitz came in and explained to the press what was going on. I don't remember how many dresses the store bought for the occasion, but I do know that it was quite a few, and we sold out.

Another innovation toward the youth market—especially the female youths—was the invention of the juniors department. Hamrick points out:

> *There was no such thing as selling to the demographic between children and adults up until then. We had an area on the third floor we called the Boutique, and that was even before the term 'boutique' was in vogue; we had it as something new. Then they opened the junior sportswear department, which was obviously for teenagers, and my boss Jo Lawley and I developed the whole program.*
>
> *No one had thought about marketing to teenagers before that. Take jeans, for example. We sold jeans at six dollars a pair, and those were brand names! At one point in the late 1960s or early 1970s, we had the Mickey Mouse t-shirts that sold by the thousands. We had Spiro Agnew t-shirts at the same time; well, Mickey Mouse sold out and we had to mark Spiro down to move those out.*

Jo Lawley concurs with her colleague:

> *The mid-1960s into the mid-1970s were the explosive years of the youth movement in many things, but especially in attitude and fashion.*

Part of Pizitz's new image in the 1960s was a concentrated marketing campaign aimed at the ever-growing teenage population. This February 1966 pamphlet teamed the newly hip Pizitz with happening radio station WAQY ("Wacky") and its top deejays. It also featured Fred Rauschenberg's relatively new Pizitz logo, which had been in use about a year and a half. *Todd Jones collection.*

Eastwood Mall had opened in August 1960 as the first such enclosed shopping mall in the South. Pizitz finally joined the Eastwood crew six years later. *Jo Lawley collection.*

Pizitz hit the curve running by realizing what was happening and creating very targeted changes in advertising, visual merchandising, special events, merchandise selection…even allowing the expanded Junior Department to break out of the typical department design to look different in wall visuals, fixtures, signing and music. As you may imagine, these drastic changes in a standard department store were not always accepted or understood by many of the traditional merchants. However it was understood and encouraged by Richard Pizitz. This aggressive youth marketing stance attracted not only national manufacturers who were rushing to catch this new lifestyle trend, but the press and national magazines as well.

All of these efforts might have been viewed as symbols of Pizitz's faith in downtown as a continuing viable retail center, but that did not mean the store was cutting back on its suburban expansion. Shopping centers, as we have seen, were among the first indicators that the city center was losing its grip, but when Eastwood Mall opened in August 1960 as the first enclosed shopping mall in the South, it was truly a marvel to behold. Even at that, Pizitz did not extend its reach to Eastwood until six years later. In August 1966, the new "Pizitz-Eastwood" (as the ads called it) opened as the fifth store in the chain, and the publicity mill was kept busy for weeks churning out newspaper ads and press releases describing it in all its $3 million glory. Shoppers gaped in slack-jawed amazement at both Eastwood Mall itself (with its "air-conditioned sidewalks" making the interior feel like "spring all year," as the publicity was fond of pointing out) and the new kid on the block, the 100,000-square-foot Pizitz store that sat at the eastern end of the mall, where previously there had been no anchor store.

And what an anchor store Pizitz dropped onto Eastwood Mall. The focus of its interior decoration was the use of different woods and colors in the different departments. The sports department was done in mission pine; the Lion's Den (men's fashions) was paneled and beamed in Viking oak and black walnut. The beauty salon had a Mexican theme, and a Spanish look prevailed in the Granada Restaurant. The escalator well was decorated with an antique pewter chandelier and a rock garden below.

The opening ceremonies for Pizitz-Eastwood served to introduce a new generation of the family to the public. Besides Isadore and Richard, who naturally presided over everything their company did, Isadore's great-grandsons Jeff and Richard Jr. were to cut the ribbon, which would be held by great-granddaughters Jill, Susan and Julie. Non-family celebrities included Newman Waters, the former movie theater impresario who had developed Eastwood Mall, newspaper editor Vincent Townsend, representing Operation New Birmingham, and the mayors of Birmingham, Mountain Brook and Irondale.

Is it beginning to seem that every time something threatened to take people's attention away from the downtown store, the most immediate reaction was to begin another remodeling program? The one instituted in 1959–60 had barely had time for the paint to dry before another top-to-bottom renovation was announced for 1966–67. As with the previous ones, it involved taking one floor at a time and completely transforming it.

Two of the most transformed floors were the top pair. The seventh floor became the home of all service offices, while the auditorium that had been on the seventh was rebuilt in the northeast corner of the sixth floor. This forty-four-foot by forty-eight-foot empty space would prove to be infinitely adaptable for a variety of uses, from enlarging the annual Enchanted Forest to hosting fashion shows to serving as a place to set up displays of larger

There are some people who think Pizitz' New Second Floor is the best one we've done yet!

We'd like your opinion, too! There's excitement everywhere on Pizitz new Second Floor! In the young, modern shops for teen boys and girls. In the handsomely appointed new Men's Store. And in the special shops for infants and children.

Hip young swingers will find nationally famous brands that give them a wide, wide choice . . . from mad to the traditional look. Thoroughly modern Minnies will love "The Flick," a nifty, knacky shop for pre-teen girls with bigger-than-life portraits of "Bogey" and other all time movie greats. In "The Student Shop," young men will find famous brands too — and the look that the leaders wear. The whole young area on the Second Floor is now, strictly upbeat all the way.

For men, there's the quiet elegance of the new Men's Store. Rich wood paneling and deep carpets provide the setting for a wide selection of nationally famous brands. Here too, is "The Lion's Den," a shop devoted to men of all ages who prefer the traditional look. Close by, a new and complete Sporting Goods Department is located.

There's excitement for mothers (grandmothers too) on the new Second Floor. They'll delight in choosing gifts and clothing from the complete infants' and children's departments. Especially from the "Playpen," an enchanting shop for baby's needs.

Yes, there's excitement all over on Pizitz' sparkling new Second Floor. Come see for yourself tomorrow!

A GUIDE TO PIZITZ SPARKLING 2ND FLOOR		
	The Flick	Children's Shoes
	Girls' World	Record Bar
	The Playpen	Sporting Goods
	Styles 2-4	Book World
	Knitwear	Camera Dept.

A major remodeling program at the downtown store occupied most of 1965–67. This full-page newspaper ad from July 26, 1967, announces the opening of the newly redecorated second floor, with such separate areas as the Flick for preteen girls, the Student Shop for young men and the Lion's Den for their fashionable elders. *Author's collection.*

appliances and toys. With its blank walls and only a single post in the very center of the room, it could become whatever the management desired.

The press release announcing the 1966–67 remodeling program gave a handy checklist of which departments would be housed on which floors:

> *The street floor will be redesigned to include men's furnishings, sportswear, shoes and hats. The second floor will now be the home of men's clothing, record, book and camera departments as well as sporting goods and boys'*

and girls' wear. The maternity wear and daytime dress departments will also be relocated to the second floor. The fifth floor will feature furniture, lamps and model rooms. The sixth floor will be the showcase for the radio and TV departments, major appliances, housewares, toys and wallpaper/paints.

Another aspect of the latest remodeling was the addition of more escalators, which previously had ended on the fourth floor. Now new sets were extended to the fifth and sixth floors, and with the new automatic elevators, customers could whisk themselves around to all the departments unlike ever before. In a letter that was sent out to all employees during the 1966 Christmas season, Richard Pizitz could practically be seen beaming through the stationery:

The mid-1960s remodeling program resulted in a new store auditorium on the sixth floor, which was often used for fashion shows such as this May 1968 one sponsored by *Ingenue* magazine. *Author's collection.*

A few days ago, I was discussing our remodeling program with a salesperson in our downtown store. He commented to me, "We've come a long way, haven't we?" I replied, "We sure have." That was the end of our conversation, but in thinking about it later, I realized just how far we have come. And I emphasize the "we" because what Pizitz is today is no more and no less than what some 1500 of us are making it. In the past few years, we have grown in size, in sales, and in reputation, and this growth has been directly due to your efforts and those of 1499 other co-workers.

So, as 1966 draws to a close, I'd like to say a very personal "thanks" to you for everything you mean to our store, and for being a part of Pizitz. We have come a long way together and I know we will continue along this path.

Pizitz's earlier aim at the youth market seemed to be the right path to follow, too, as the late 1960s saw that culture—or, in some cases, counterculture—reaching new levels of influence in society. Historian Hal Lifson was specifically commenting on the year 1966 when he wrote, "Teen culture was the overriding social theme of the decade. Television shows, fashion and music were all targeted to the youth market, and it was the first time in modern history that adults really took on the same interests as their children."

With this attitude permeating pop culture, Pizitz's next step should have come as no surprise to anyone. Again, let's see what Jo Lawley can tell us about it:

This explosive new trend created a wave of new youth magazines with SEVENTEEN magazine taking a prominent lead. The marketing of this fast-moving trend required teen-oriented special events like choreographed fashion shows with rock music, bright colors and modern psychedelic designs, bikinis, hot pants, and short-short skirts...the shorter the better! The editors at SEVENTEEN put together a group of department stores across the country that had the marketing plan and the budget to exploit this "happening." SEVENTEEN offered special regional advertising rates, sent guest editors for fashion shows and to appear with the store on TV interviews. From this partnership with SEVENTEEN, "Teen Boards" were formed in approximately 30 department stores across the country.

The format was for each store to create a Teen Board of juniors or seniors from every high school in their marketing area. The qualifications were beauty, personality and top grades, and hundreds of girls came for personal interviews made up from a panel of judges from the community.

Each year Pizitz selected between 16 and 20 girls who were assigned to be key participants in fashion shows, workshops, community events and were featured in some of the newspaper advertising. The most coveted prize was the girl who was selected to go to Market Week in New York to compete with other Teen Board members from across the country, and SEVENTEEN would select a National SEVENTEEN Teen Board of 12 girls to be featured in a special edition of the magazine. In the late sixties, the Pizitz Teen Board candidate Sharon Wall was one of the finalists.

The SEVENTEEN Teen Board was one of the most successful national marketing plans during this historic period because it gave the stores a national marketing umbrella, national advertising for a regional store, and a group of beautiful young girls to represent the store in the local communities. Pizitz was one of the stores who gave a scholarship to the top Teen Board member.

All of these sales promotions were part of Fred Rauschenberg's territory, and his co-workers are unanimous in saddling him with such adjectives as "talented," "creative" and "a unique personality." Or, as Jo Lawley elaborates: "Fred worked 24/7 in the office or at home. In fact, he built a complete advertising office adjacent to his garage and it was very common for him to call me, or any merchant, over a weekend to come to his house to work on a campaign. Everyone loved and admired Fred because of his talent, his intrepid enthusiasm and understanding of merchandise; and his ability to make something happen."

Before Rauschenberg lit out for the West Coast to become vice-president and sales promotion manager for the May Company department stores, he came up with another idea: a Pizitz Block Party for teens. "That was unheard of at the time," Sharon Hamrick says, "because he took the downtown store and opened all six floors to teenagers for one big after-hours party. They had rock bands, they had dancing, they had all the radio DJ's and TV personalities there…it was just one big event for teenagers. The kids came downtown and took over the store. That had never been heard of, but it worked!"

The path toward expanding the number of Pizitz stores grew wider in September 1967, when Isadore and his comrades announced that the sixth store in the chain would open the following year at the Five Points West shopping center. The details of that particular branch graphically illustrate the changing styles in retailing. The first portions of Five Points West had opened in 1941, but it was in the late 1950s that it grew into what most

Pizitz opened its Five Points West branch on August 22, 1968. Whereas Five Points West had previously been a standard open-air shopping center, the addition of Pizitz at the rear created a miniature mall to bring the facility up to date with modern shopping standards. Notice that Pizitz replicated one of the main features of its downtown store with another parking deck and skywalk entrance. *Author's collection.*

people would consider a true shopping center. The new two-story Pizitz store was to be built behind the existing strip, and to connect it with the other stores, an enclosed mall was to be built through the center of the older structures. From that point on, Five Points West would be an odd hybrid of mall and shopping center, with Pizitz as the focal point at the rear. Actually, the articles pointed out that "Pizitz-West" was a *three*-story structure, with the bottom floor a parking garage. An escalator would carry shoppers from the cavernous space up into the new mall. The Five Points West Pizitz development also included a new parking deck, styled after the downtown one that was still garnering praise; like downtown, the deck would connect to the new Pizitz store via a skywalk.

Your Store

The new store opened on schedule in August 1968. It turned out to be the same size as the Eastwood Mall store, 100,000 square feet, and the interior decoration was much the same. The escalators in the center of the store were again overlooked by a spectacular chandelier. As one might expect, men's, women's and children's clothing could be found on the first floor (or second floor, if you count the ground-level parking garage as the first floor), while on the second floor (or third floor—confusing, isn't it?) there were home furnishings, housewares, domestics, sporting goods, a beauty salon and a toy department that was decorated in the same motif as the one on the sixth floor downtown.

Pizitz's influence also extended to the mall area that was built to service it. Thousands of former shoppers remember the gushing fountain that sat in front of the Pizitz entrance, providing a restful area to sit and relax. Much care and attention were given to Pizitz's display windows that faced the mall's interior, and the soft green glow of the neon that illuminated the distinctive Pizitz script logo was a large part of the store's appealing appearance.

Paperwork exists from that same month the Five Points West store opened to show the sort of planning involved in staging a big publicity event downtown, which, after all, was still the flagship store. On August 10, NFL players Johnny Unitas and Gayle Sayers were to make a personal appearance in the second-floor boys' department, and a stack of inter-office memos shows just how all the different parts of the store were to work together to make things happen. Advertising was taken out in both the *Birmingham News* and *Birmingham Post-Herald*, with radio spots airing on WJLD, WENN, WSGN and WBRC. Michael Pizitz's responsibility was to arrange the pickup and return of the football heroes from their respective hotels (Unitas was at the Sheraton Motor Inn and Sayers at the Guest House), and 1,500 autographed photos and two thousand pinback buttons were to be ordered. The two gridiron giants were to receive $300 each for their appearances— an amount for which an NFL star of the twenty-first century probably would not even make a phone call.

Joe Dultz would be responsible for creating an appropriate display window on Second Avenue, as well as a platform in the boys' department on which the two guests could make their appearance. Security was to provide two policemen on the second floor for crowd control, and photographer Bill Ivey was given specific instructions for shots he was to get: the players entering the store via the skywalk, crowd shots of Unitas and Sayers talking to children and so on. What is amazing is that this sort of thing went on for every special event the store put on—and there were a number of them each year.

This would be one of the last such frenzies for Joe Dultz, who retired in November 1968. His replacement was Jim Luker, formerly of Ivey's department store (no relation to Bill Ivey!) in Jacksonville, Florida. Luker would direct Pizitz's display department and visual merchandising for the rest of the chain's life, and then some. As we are about to learn in the next chapter, he arrived just in time to see that year's version of the Enchanted Forest, and he would soon begin formulating plans to expand it beyond anything Dultz had ever imagined.

Chapter 5

CHRISTMAS ENCHANTMENT

E ven though department stores' decorated Christmas windows were a long-established and cherished tradition, there was one major flaw in them from a business perspective. Namely, that was that people remained *outside* the store to look at them. By the early 1960s, retailers in various parts of the country were beginning to rethink the wisdom of that and come up with ways to make Christmas work harder for them.

At about the same time, another problem reared its head in how to entertain the long lines of children waiting for their turn on Santa Claus's lap. In larger stores, the wait could seem interminable, which frayed the nerves of both the kids and their parents. One solution was to turn the waiting line into an attraction of its own, usually named as some variation of "Santa Land," in which animated figures and other Christmas scenery gave everyone something to look at while gearing up for an audience with the jolly old elf.

These two approaches converged at Pizitz in 1964, and what resulted is widely regarded as another of Fred Rauschenberg's brainy brainstorms. Newspaper readers the week before Thanksgiving were confronted by a full-page ad announcing something new: something called the Enchanted Forest, which could be seen on Pizitz's sixth floor. The description made it sound like the momentous event it really was:

> *The moment you enter this winter wonderland, you're caught in a magic spell of fantasy. It's breathtakingly beautiful with twinkling stars, frosty trees, animated teddy bears and all the enchantment of Christmas, created*

This ad ran in the newspaper the week before Thanksgiving 1964. It announced the first appearance of the Enchanted Forest, an annual Christmas tradition at Pizitz for the next twenty years. *Author's collection.*

by our own talented craftsmen. It has taken months to assemble, and we feel sure you've never seen anything like it.

Most of that was true and would still be true almost twenty years later. The untold fact, however, was that the original Enchanted Forest came to Pizitz secondhand, as it were. The scenes depicting a village of living teddy bears had already spent several Christmas seasons at the Maison Blanche department store in New Orleans, where, according to some of those citizens' vague memories, it had also been known as the Enchanted Forest. Joe Dultz had brought the pieces of the display to Birmingham, and the idea of placing it on the sixth floor was to be sure shoppers had to pass through the lower five floors of merchandise to get to it. As we have seen, in 1964 Pizitz's escalators had not yet been extended above the fourth floor, and self-service elevators were about six months away, so those who wanted to tour the forest during its inaugural year had to make a bit of an effort to get there.

Another thing that did not exist in 1964 was the large sixth-floor auditorium. The question of just where the forest was placed under those circumstances is difficult for even the Pizitz family to answer after so many years, but the general consensus is that since the original Forest setup was rather small, an area near the housewares department was temporarily walled off for the season, and that was where the snow fell and bears frolicked. Hearkening back to other stores' camouflaging of the Santa waiting line, old St. Nick hung out at the end of the forest trail, ready to make his list and check it twice.

Apparently in the beginning, the whole forest was built around the Maison Blanche bears. There were shopping bears, bears trying to extricate their car that had become stuck in the snow, a "Bearber Shop" and the "Honey Hotel" (no doubt a play on the term "Honeymoon Hotel"). The display's designers were a bear for punishment when it came to puns—even the most grizzly ones.

The original version of the Enchanted Forest was built around a village of living teddy bears. This "peek-a-boo" bear was brought out of retirement in 1973 to once again peer at shoppers along the forest path. *Author's collection.*

The bears remained the focal point during the first two or three years of the forest's existence. Newspaper ads indicate that by 1966, they had been joined by "the merry snowmen skating" and "the polar bears cavorting down slides," hinting that perhaps the display was growing a bit more complex. The sixth-floor auditorium was completed in early 1967, so it is logical to presume that the forest moved into those new quarters during that Christmas season. At the same time, the toy department was moved from its long-standing home on the second floor up to the sixth, probably to take advantage of what was going to be a very happy case of Christmas synergy.

As we saw in the previous chapter, Joe Dultz retired and Jim Luker was hired as his replacement during November 1968. Luker later remembered seeing that year's forest for the first time and realizing that it was going to be his responsibility beginning in 1969. "They only had about five scenes, or groups of animated characters," he recalled. "In between those scenes was nothing but snow and frosty trees. I knew I wanted to do something so that no matter where a person looked, there was something to see."

In 1968, the Enchanted Forest moved away from its former "teddy bears" theme and became the home to Santa Claus and all his helpers. Along with the animated animals, the elves could be seen making toys, grooming the reindeer and otherwise making preparations for the big day. *Author's collection.*

Luker said that the forest as he originally saw it was occupying only about two-thirds of the auditorium. It had taken on a slightly different flavor in 1968, too, as the original bears were phased out and scenes of Santa's elves and reindeer were brought in to replace them. The ads that year served as a checklist of the new theme: "SEE the little elves in their candy kitchens preparing Christmas goodies! WATCH the cascading waterfall and the little goldfish swimming! LOOK at the elves as they stitch 'n' sew away! VISIT Santa's stables—see the reindeer being groomed and curried for their big ride!"

By this time, most of the Maison Blanche bears—which, remember, had been purchased used to begin with—had been retired. Keeping the older figures running was sometimes a frustrating job in itself, Luker said. "Many of the mechanisms were made in Germany, and there just was nowhere in the United

Beginning in 1969, Pizitz's display director, Jim Luker, was the guiding force behind the Enchanted Forest. He often said that it was his favorite project of the year, and his care and interest showed clearly in the finished product. *Luker family collection.*

States that could repair them if they stopped working." In some cases, the motors were placed underneath the raised twelve-inch platform on which the forest was built; in others, the mechanisms were hidden in snowbanks and underneath foliage.

By 1970, Luker had managed to expand the forest's outer boundaries to the very walls of the auditorium, giving him plenty of space with which to work. Even at that, he had to observe limitations. The fire code specified that the auditorium could have an occupancy of only a finite number of people, whether they were seated in chairs or standing in a twisting forest path, so Luker had to be sure that the total number of people in line would not

These fastidious snowmen were first seen in the 1970 Enchanted Forest and went on to become annual favorites. Jim Luker would attend trade shows soon after the first of each year, carefully inspecting the newest releases in department store animated figures. *Author's collection.*

exceed that number. There was also the matter of making sure all materials in the forest were nonflammable, since the motors and their attendant wires were underneath the snow. No one wanted a repeat of the 1959 display window incident in a room densely packed with people.

This concern for safety, as well as plain old economics, meant that every mechanical figure received close inspection after each year's forest was dismantled. If Luker felt the motor was in good enough shape to serve for another season, the figure could be counted on to appear again. If the motor was deficient but the character still looked presentable, Luker would use the figure as a motionless decoration somewhere along the path, sometimes placing it on a turntable to give the illusion of movement where there actually was none. For a few years, the flow of the forest path was interrupted by what was labeled as an "icy bridge" over a frozen stream, and some of the nonanimated animals could be seen standing along this snowy riverbank.

Of course, we should not forget that as the display director, Luker had other Christmas responsibilities in addition to the forest. Among those was seeing that the outside of the Pizitz building was suitably decked out to delight all those holiday shoppers. The year Luker arrived, Joe Dultz had just acquired a multistory Christmas tree fashioned from strands of tinsel that would adorn the corner of the building. It was impressive in its scope, but Luker was not especially pleased with its color: the tinsel was gold, which faded into the terra cotta surface of the building. For 1969, he had the corner tree reworked with tinsel that was not only green but a blindingly loud green. Lights were intertwined with the tinsel, and the tree supported some huge illuminated candles that were almost fluorescent red. There was no way anyone could ignore that tree, and besides, Luker said he was enough of a traditionalist to believe Christmas trees should always be green, rather than gold or any other kooky color.

The forest was still the major annual design job. Luker said that he generally began working on the next year's forest as soon as Christmas was over—sometimes sooner, as he would make notes while the display was up and running each season. Soon after the New Year, he would attend display shows in New York and Chicago to check out the latest models in animated figures, and by June he would have his budget ready for approval by the Pizitz family. That was something that did not concern him too much, as Isadore was probably the biggest fan the forest ever had. "Every year, after we got it set up and before we opened it to the public, Mr. Isadore insisted on being the first person to walk through," Luker recalled. "He loved it. He would always come out smiling and shaking his head in amazement."

The actual manual labor would begin in October, when the auditorium would be closed off for any other use and the workers would begin erecting the platform that formed the shape of the path. Even before then,

The Talking Christmas Tree was introduced in 1971. Members of Pizitz's Teen Board were recruited to sit inside and converse with passing children, whom they could see through the two-way mirrors that formed the tree's eyes. *Author's collection.*

Luker and his assistants would have already begun hauling the past years' supply of animated figures out of the warehouse, unwrapping them from their careful packing and checking each one to see if it were still usable.

Some elements of the forest were built on site rather than purchased from display companies. At one of the trade shows Luker attended, someone was promoting a rolling Christmas tree that could roam a store and talk to customers. Pizitz's aisles were too narrow and crowded for that to be an option, but it gave Luker an idea. When he got home, he drew up plans for a hollow Talking Christmas Tree for the 1971 forest. Members of Pizitz's Teen Board were recruited to serve as the tree's operator; the tree was basically a huge puppet with the mouth controlled by a foot pedal instead of a puppeteer's hand. Luker held auditions for Teen Board members to determine which ones had the most talent for synchronizing their voices with the foot pedal. The Talking Tree had eyes fashioned from mirrors, so the girls inside could see the crowd, but people standing in front of the tree saw only their own reflections. Fortunately, the auditorium's back wall had a door already made into it, which served as a dandy way for the tree's operators to enter and leave unseen.

The tree's arrival coincided with someone else's departure. Having Santa at the end of the trail made for a memorable grand finale, but it did cause the waiting line to sometimes back up to a standstill. The solution was to move the live Santa to another part of the sixth floor and leave the tree as the only conversationalist in the forest. To make sure a similar event did not occur, the path widened to almost double its usual size in front of the tree, so those who did not wish to prattle with a pine could go on about their business.

The Talking Christmas Tree created something of a sensation in the Pizitz world. It was such a hit downtown that additional versions of it were eventually installed in the Huntsville, Gadsden, Florence and Montgomery stores. Actually, newspaper ads for the newly opened downtown Montgomery Pizitz in 1972 invited everyone to "see Santa in his Enchanted Forest on the third floor," so for at least one year there was an attempt to recreate the walk-through forest in that location. For the most part, though, the tree would merely be set up in front of a six-foot-wide backdrop, allowing the operator some privacy to make entrances and exits.

The 1972 forest was heavily promoted as "all new," with Santa's big move as only one of the features. There was an updated entrance gate made of simulated stained glass. The path now contained an "ice cave" halfway through, curving around the auditorium's center support pole and lighted

The 1972 newspaper ads made much of the fact that the Enchanted Forest was "all new" for that year. Except for the Talking Christmas Tree, nothing in the display had ever been seen before. *Author's collection.*

inside by twinkling colored Christmas bulbs. Another novel sight, which was trotted out every other year or so, was the Magic Mirror, in which one object could be seen "changing" into another. The effect was quite simple but required some extremely skilled design. Basically, one figure was being viewed as a reflection in the mirror while the other was behind the glass and became visible when a spotlight shone on it. A newspaper ad from that year spelled out some of the other new features:

> *Santa's helpers are busily preparing an old-fashioned Christmas in their enchanting forest filled with twirling gumdrop trees and fresh white show, where a friendly Christmas tree actually talks to you and a magic spot gives you a peek at Santa waving and changing into a beautiful pear-trimmed tree, right before your eyes! A fountain gurgles, lights twinkle, children from all lands ride a Ferris wheel and ski and bake and cook and rock and swing and have a grand time entertaining you.*

The Enchanted Forest's "new look" involved a heavy infusion of realistic human figures, which threatened to take the spotlight away from Santa's staff and their animal companions. These skiing children, part of the 1972 makeover, were examples of this more humanized approach. *Author's collection.*

If you think hard enough, you may recall that 1973 was the year President Richard Nixon threw a grinch into the nation's Christmas celebration by discouraging people from decorating their houses and lawns, due to a perceived shortage of electricity. Whether or not Pizitz necessarily agreed with this edict, the store did take some steps during that season to at least give the impression of being a team player. A press release singled out the giant Christmas tree on the corner, stating that its lights would "twinkle brightly from 5 p.m. 'til 10 p.m. only, instead of from twilight to midnight." Lights in the display windows, and all other outdoor lighting, would also be turned off at 10:00 p.m. The lights inside the store would be turned on ten minutes before opening and turned off ten minutes after closing; the same time frame applied to the escalators. Lamps and television sets in the furniture departments would be turned on only to demonstrate them for customers. Noticeably, nothing was said about the electricity needed to power the dozens of animated figures and hundreds of lights in the Enchanted Forest.

By the mid-1970s, the forest had gotten about as far away from its early bears-and-elves format as possible. Animated figures had been getting more and more lifelike all along. The 1972 ad had hinted at this trend with its emphasis on "children of all lands," but by 1975, human characters outnumbered animals and elves to an alarming degree. Some of the backdrops for the scenes even depicted city streets instead of foliage, making the Enchanted Forest name seem a bit out of place. A major overhaul in 1976 restored the forest theme, and 1977 saw the Talking Tree replaced with a pair of talking reindeer, namely Rudolph and Vixen. Unlike the tree, which Luker had had to design from the seeds up, as it were, the reindeer were a preexisting display item. Now either one or two performers at a time could take their places inside the stable and carry on conversations with visitors, as well as with each other. The deer duet was controlled by rods that moved their mouths and could turn their bodies back and forth, but other than that, their motions were almost as limited as that of the stationary tree.

In the December 1976 issue of the store newsletter, *Pizitz Pen Points*, employee Rosebelle Greenberg commented on the role the forest played in each year's celebration:

> *My favorite article for Christmas at Pizitz is, you guessed it, the Enchanted Forest. This year, some new and exciting changes were made and the Enchanted Forest on the sixth floor of the downtown store is more like a fairyland—more enchanting and a thing of beauty to behold. Thanks again go to Jim Luker and his coworkers in the display department.*
>
> *Everyone has an invitation to see the Enchanted Forest of 1976. Please join the wonderful world of kids, and you too will be oohing and aahing with them! The beautiful spirit of Christmas in our hearts never really changes. Our eyes meet, we smile that secret, happy, knowing smile together and go our separate ways, feeling joyously uplifted as the wonderful memory of peace on earth, good will to men prevails.*

The forest remained as complex as ever, but by 1980, the crowds of downtown shoppers were just no longer there. In that year, the forest's path and general look were completely redone once again, this time to convey what Luker described as "a more liberating, fantasy approach." Much of this was due to the design work of Luker's assistant, Martha Haarbauer, who added such unusual touches as having springtime flowers growing out of the snow. Haarbauer was very active in Birmingham's theater community, and that background showed clearly in her 1980 revamping of the forest. Giant set pieces were a far cry from Maison-Blanche's teddy bears, and one scene full of dragons and wizards took the whole Enchanted Forest concept in a sword-and-sorcery direction that was prevalent in pop culture of the era. Even that could not have prepared the few remaining forest visitors for what they were going to see in 1981, though.

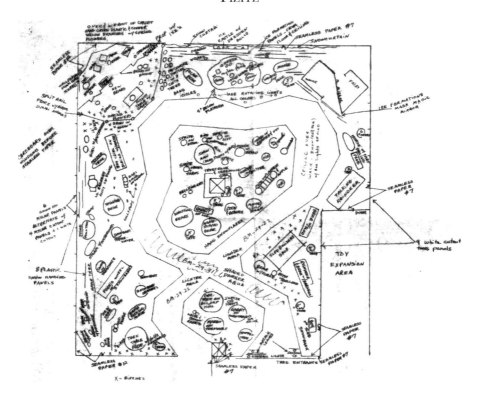

Martha Haarbauer drew this floor plan for the 1980 Enchanted Forest. It is evident that she threw everything she could into this year's display, which would be the next to last time it would inhabit the sixth-floor auditorium. *Author's collection.*

Charles Elliott had recently joined the display staff, and he says that for that year, they decided to capitalize on the craze for science fiction movies such as *Star Wars* by taking "the Enchanted Forest into the future." Walking the trail, customers were hemmed in by a stretchy material known in the display world as "space fabric." Futuristic it did seem, but the only animated figures that could be seen had to be glimpsed through "portholes" in the fabric. Some of these windows were at adult height and others at child level nearer to the floor, but each revealed only a small vignette. The post in the center of the auditorium, which had been disguised as everything from a cave stalagmite to a giant tree, now became a space ship. "I had nothing to do with designing the new entrance," Elliott recalls, "but they used black and dark green mesh, with limbs covered in fake Spanish moss. It looked more like a haunted, wicked tree type of entrance, although once you got inside you only saw the space fabric with the portholes in it." Whatever this forest mutation was intended to do, it was the last time the forest inhabited the auditorium.

From 1982 through the 1986 Christmas season, the forest returned to its roots and appeared only as a setup in Pizitz's corner window. At the time, Luker commented on this change: "Someone said that the danger of becoming too modern is that you will suddenly find that you are very old-fashioned! 25 years ago it was very 'in' to install animated windows, so this year, management decided to try something NEW and do it again. That is the nature of our business."

The Talking Reindeer were retained for the earliest of those years and, through the puppetry and voice work of Earle Capellen, who had been with the display staff since 1974, continued to carry on conversations with the people on the sidewalk via a loudspeaker. Most of the animated figures not needed for the window had been sold off or given away; among the survivors were some penguins that had first appeared in the 1975 forest. They ended

This moose, which debuted in the 1976 forest and lasted through the display's years as a scene in Pizitz's corner window, now spends his retirement years in a local museum of pop culture artifacts. *Author's collection.*

up as part of the display in Century Plaza's center court. A few of the more recent additions were purchased by Ed's Pet World in Homewood. Another relic was a huge animated moose, probably the largest single figure the forest ever had, not counting the Talking Tree and Talking Reindeer. The moose spent more than twenty years in a Birmingham collector's den before being purchased for a local museum of pop culture artifacts, where he still lives today.

Considering that the forest, in an ever-growing form, occupied the auditorium for eighteen Christmases and then the corner window for six more years, it is somewhat surprising that more photographic documentation of it has not survived. Most people obviously did not think to bring cameras and flashbulbs with them when shopping at Pizitz, but even official publicity photographs are nonexistent. It is almost as if the forest really was what it appeared to be: a fantastic dream world that can be enjoyed in memory but never captured for posterity. But those of us who saw it with our own eyes can be positive that it really existed—or can we?

Chapter 6

BRANCHING OUT

The 1970s at Pizitz started off good enough to eat—literally. For a few years, Pizitz had contracted with Birmingham's legendary Marsh Bakeries to operate bake counters in the downtown, Roebuck and Eastwood Mall stores. However, by 1969, Marsh was undergoing some financial reverses, and after about a year of trying to keep the in-store bake shops in operation, Pizitz saw that it needed to send for an expert.

The baking whiz it brought in was Kurt Hertrich, a Swiss chef who had been dishing up his goodies at the Statler Hotel in New York City and then at the Joseph Horne department store in Pittsburgh. Hertrich brought with him the Pennsylvania Dutch tradition of baking, much of which was new to the former Confederate States. Hertrich says:

> *Back in 1970, the bakery market here was very limited…you had the coconut cakes, the potato pies and the carrot cakes and that was about it. People didn't know what an egg layer was back then. We went into pastries, brownies and many, many kinds of cakes. Birthday cakes and wedding cakes were our biggest market.*
>
> *We developed a new filling for birthday cakes that used maraschino cherries and pecans. Originally we filled the middle layer with that, and the two outer layers with lemon butter cream. That's another thing that was not known down here; we split the layers with multi-flavors.*

In 1970, Kurt Hertrich was brought in to head up the Pizitz Bake Shops. His background as a Swiss pastry chef soon caused the bake shops to expand outside the Pizitz stores into an entire chain throughout northern Alabama. *Kurt Hertrich collection.*

A press release from the same era used a bit more overblown language to say the same thing:

> *Kurt Hertrich has revolutionized the taste buds of Alabama with his mouth-watering Black Forest Cake and Bavarian Crème Torte. Everyone's talking about the fragrant, tender, crunchy French bread and rolls, the crisp cookies, the buttery streusels! And the wedding cakes are so beautiful, brides cry when they have to cut them, but guests know how good the butter cake tastes and insist on their slice.*

Whatever Hertrich was doing, it met with the hearty approval of Birmingham's sweet tooth crowd. "We ended up with 18 bake shops in Birmingham, and 26 counting the other cities…Florence, Decatur, Huntsville, Gadsden, Tuscaloosa, Montgomery. We actually started out within the stores, but it was so successful that we started opening independent ones."

Birthday cakes and wedding cakes were among the biggest-selling products of the Pizitz Bake Shops. At one point, Hertrich had to keep the central bakery running twenty-four hours a day just to meet the demand. *Dennis Campbell collection.*

In an even more unusual move, in 1973 Pizitz installed a bake shop in the downtown Sears store and another when the Sears at Century Plaza opened the following year. To keep up with the demand, Hertrich was responsible for a bakery in a warehouse at Second Avenue and Second Street, where he kept operations going twenty-four hours a day to meet orders.

At the downtown store, the main bake shop was on the street floor, of course, but many people have fond memories of the smaller counter that was located in the space between the parking deck elevators and the skywalk into the third floor. Anyone entering or leaving the store via that route could not help being assaulted by the delicious smells of freshly baked cookies and cakes. That counter was intended primarily for impulse buying as shoppers headed back to their cars, as few people would have been inclined to buy sweets and carry them around with them during their visit to the store—but having the skywalk bake counter be the first and last thing encountered was a surefire way to start their stomachs growling.

One annual occasion that brought shoppers into the store, and past the bake counter, was spring break. Now, if you have lived in Alabama for any length of time, you probably know that it was not called spring break in those days. Instead, it was "AEA Week," designated thus because it was the week when every teacher in the state converged on Birmingham for five days of meetings conducted by the Alabama Education Association. With kids out of school, not to mention the spouses accompanying the teachers, Birmingham would polish up its biggest apple for them and prepare for the major economical impact that they brought. In the early 1970s, Pizitz developed a pattern of building a "theme" for each AEA week, which would be carried out throughout the store.

In 1970 and 1971, the overall theme was the southern California lifestyle, something that most Alabamians had only seen depicted in the movies or on television. West Coast fashions were modeled on the third floor, native California foods were available on the first floor, the mezzanine restaurant served Mexican and Forty-Niner dishes, the fifth floor featured a "hacienda" room displaying furniture and accessories patterned after the Mexican-Spanish motif and on the fourth floor there was a re-creation of Muscle Beach, with young gymnasts showing off their physiques. (That last exhibit presumably featured only males, since girls' sports still had a long way to go to catch up.) The main floor had a fake ice-skating rink sponsored by DuPont, coated with Teflon rather than ice, on which skaters swirled around to the strains of recorded music.

However, each year also had a subtext of sorts. For 1970, with the Birmingham release of the animated feature *A Boy Named Charlie Brown* in the offing, the *Peanuts* characters served as the store's mascots for AEA Week. "Lucy's Lemonade Stand" on the second floor dispensed "a free glass of lemonade and some psychiatric advice," as the ads cryptically phrased it. That floor was also the locale for "Red Baron Headquarters," where a costumed Snoopy hung out among impressive displays of *Peanuts* merchandise that could now fill a museum. Kids ages ten and under were encouraged to bring their own drawings of Snoopy for a contest to win a six-foot-tall stuffed replica of the famous beagle.

For 1971, the California theme was supplemented by a "jungle safari" flavor, tying in with Los Angeles's famous Lion Country Safari attraction. (A year or two later, a less successful Lion Country Safari opened near Atlanta, making one wonder if this were not part of a "test market" of sorts.) One of the special guests during that week was Eva Gabor, of the soon-to-be-canceled *Green Acres* situation comedy, who appeared alongside some of her own brand-name wigs in Pizitz's third-floor Wig Salon. Adults might have been surprised to see Ms. Gabor at Pizitz, dahling, but among the other safari-related activities was one that made some kids do a double take.

So entrenched was the Enchanted Forest every Christmas that children could be seen peering into the empty auditorium at other times of the year, as if they expected to see Santa and his elves spending their summer vacations in there. Well, during AEA Week 1971, the forest path did indeed appear out of season, as part of the jungle theme. But instead of snow and frosty trees, the foliage was lush and green, with artificial palm trees and tropical flowers everywhere. Many of the same animated animals (the non-polar ones, of course) were part of the temporary setup. In a pen, attractive hostesses from Lion Country Safari proudly showed off a pair of three-month-old lion cubs.

COME ON SAFARI . . . Adventure into the unknown and thrill to the mysterious! Explore California from the exotic lush and foliage of the jungle trail in our 6th floor auditorium to the gastronomic delights of The Grotto, patterned after Fisherman's Wharf restaurants! Ooh and aah over the cuddly lion cubs and their adorable trainers from Lion Country Safari! See the latest and adventuresome fashions modeled daily! Register for thousands of dollars worth of free prizes, including a Safari for 2 to the West Coast via Delta at our Delta Booth, Street Floor Downtown, all week—March 15-20!

AEA Week, which is now known as spring break, was always an opportunity for a major sales promotion at Pizitz. For 1971, the theme was a "California Safari," and in the sixth-floor auditorium, Jim Luker's display staff brought out the usual Enchanted Forest setup and turned it into an African jungle. *Author's collection.*

As mentioned in an earlier chapter, the only permanent structure in the auditorium was a post in the very center of the room. This post had to be camouflaged in various creative ways during the annual forest, but it had its part to play during the Jungle Safari too. A cage surrounding the post bore a sign reading, "Look inside to see the monkey." When shoppers stooped down to look inside, they saw their own reflection in a mirror mounted on the post. Jim Luker and his staff must have been laughing their heads off when they came up with that idea.

This page: These photos of an April 1971 fashion show in the auditorium, hosted by Channel 42 TV personality Sergeant Jack (Neal Miller), were taken just a few weeks after the California Safari jungle had been dismantled. Notice that the room was a totally blank slate that could be adapted for any purpose. The curtained door at far left was the rear entrance for the girls who performed the Talking Christmas Tree. *Luker family collection.*

By the early 1970s, AEA Week was only one of a whole line of special events put on by Pizitz. A press release enumerated several of them, which were in addition to the springtime and Yuletide festivities:

SEVENTEEN BEAUTY WORKS—Special charm and beauty courses offered twice a year at Pizitz for teenage girls.

WHITE GLOVES AND PARTY MANNERS—A charm course for little girls ages 5 to 15 is offered twice a year.

ALL-AMERICAN TRACK MEET—Sponsored by Buster Brown Textiles, Pizitz and the Police Athletic League of Birmingham to promote track and field events for elementary school students.

BEAUTIFUL ACTIVISTS—A special recognition program sponsored by Pizitz and Germaine Montell. This is a statewide event designed to salute women for their work in their community, city, state or nation.

FALL FASHION WEEK—A special week-long promotion in August with daily fashion shows, guest designers and approximately 18 pages of new fall fashion newspaper advertising.

IN-STORE FASHION EVENTS for women's clubs held in sixth floor auditorium with catered luncheons.

BRIDAL FAIR—Twice a year with WSGN Radio; special bridal shows, panel discussions, gift and bakery displays at the City Auditorium.

The above-mentioned Fall Fashion Week prompted these memories of one particular year's event from Jo Lawley:

It was called "Fashion Under The Stars," and Jim Luker designed the top of the parking deck with thousands of twinkling lights and roving flood lights. Eight antique cars on the next level down brought the models up two or three at a time…producing a dramatic live fashion show while cocktails and hors d'oeuvres were passed out by waiters and waitresses in black and white uniforms. Because this was the opening of the citywide Fall Fashion Week, Pizitz had guest designers and manufacturers as our guests and they were dazzled! A very special guest, a millinery designer and new on the fashion scene, was Halston, who became an international celebrity designer. Years later I saw him in the market and we reminisced about the uniqueness of the event and how lucky we were because it was a clear, starry night.

Another big event each year was the semi-annual Sample Sale. What was that, you may well ask? We will let Sharon Hamrick explain, as she was right in the thick (or maybe thin) of it:

> *This was a big deal in the juniors and sportswear departments. The buyers, including me, would go to New York and buy a line of clothes from the samples in the showrooms. And if you wore a size nine in juniors…all samples were the same size…or a size ten in misses, you could get the most incredible forward fashions for forty percent off—which at that time was a drop-dead price. People would line up in the skywalk coming into the third floor, and when the dressing rooms would be full, ladies would start stripping to their underwear in the middle of the sales floor to try on the outfits!*

Sort of gives a whole new meaning to "40 percent off," doesn't it?

In the midst of all this underdressed excitement, March 1971 was the month of a major announcement for Birmingham. It received the designation of an "All America City," which was looked upon as something of a miracle considering the turmoil in which it had found itself not even ten years earlier. This was an honor conferred by *Look* magazine upon cities judged to have met the proper criteria. All businesses and organizations in Birmingham jumped on the "All America City" honor as a highly coveted prize, but Richard Pizitz came in for his share of the glory as president of the chamber of commerce. He was the one who traveled to *Look*'s home turf

WBRC-TV's Pat Gray loaned her striking beauty to a fashion show on Pizitz's third floor around 1973. *Pat Gray collection.*

of Portland, Oregon, in company with representative Betty Cox and civil rights leader Chris McNair, to plead the case for Birmingham to receive this designation. Donald A. Brown, the editor of the chamber's publication, *Birmingham* magazine, said of Richard, "I don't give him all the credit. Just most of it. As Chamber president, Pizitz signed Birmingham's original application. The letters stating that we were an All America City came to his home. This Chamber today, this All America City, at the very least owes Dick Pizitz a thank you and well-done."

(Proving that by this time, historical perspective was skewed beyond all possible hope, in December 1971 Pizitz had begun the celebration of its seventy-fifth anniversary—despite the fact that it would be another two and a half years before that milestone arrived.)

A less significant but highly touted Pizitz event in late 1971 and early 1972 was the store's association with an ABC-TV Saturday morning

From fall 1971 until spring 1972, Pizitz promoted the merchandise from an ABC-TV Saturday morning show known as *Curiosity Shop*. A portion of the second floor was converted into an approximation of the show's set, and the characters appeared on a wide variety of toys and children's clothes. *Luker family collection.*

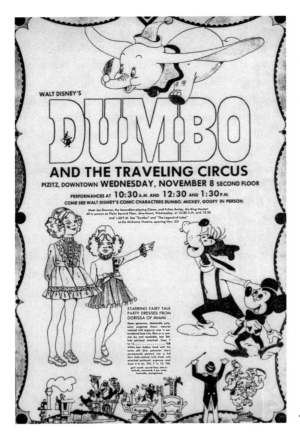

After the opening of Walt Disney World in Florida in October 1971, Pizitz often ran promotional activities tied in with the Disney company. This November 1972 ad announced the arrival of Mickey Mouse, Goofy, Dumbo and the rest of the Fantasyland gang. *Jo Lawley collection.*

children's show called *Curiosity Shop*. We know you have probably never heard of it. The program was conceived as a sort of *Sesame Street* for grade schoolers rather than preschoolers and was a production of famed animator Chuck Jones. It starred an appealing cast mix of live children (including the secret crush of many boys, teen actress Pamelyn Ferdin), oversized puppets, animated characters and other disparate elements. Pizitz snagged a deal to be the official Birmingham headquarters for *Curiosity Shop* merchandise, and Jim Luker set about turning a section of the second floor into an area themed around the show's props and characters. By the spring of 1972, the dismal ratings had proven conclusively that the TV show was a total failure, and Pizitz quietly swept away any mention of it. Today, it is next to impossible to find any of the varied lines of character merchandise Pizitz sold during that brief experiment.

It was not Luker's fault that *Curiosity Shop* failed to catch on the way the Enchanted Forest had, but it was the overall body of his work that prompted the National Association of the Display Industry (NADI) to present him with its annual award in December 1973. As the press release put it, "The NADI awards this 'Oscar' to members of their profession whose efforts show the most originality, professional polish and all-around excellence." On behalf of Pizitz, Luker was presented with the award for stores with an annual volume of less than $100 million. (His winning counterpart among the big boys was the display department head for Chicago's Marshall Field's.)

By that time, Pizitz was up to seven stores and counting. The chain had opened its first store in Montgomery on downtown's Dexter Avenue in April 1972. One might naturally suppose that such an urban location would mean that Pizitz stepped into an older store's building; one would be wrong. Montgomery had been undergoing a major urban renewal project at the time, with antique buildings being demolished right and left, and Pizitz was able to snag a vacant lot and build its own new store literally from the ground up.

Plans were on the drawing board for two more branches, Gadsden and Birmingham's new Brookwood Village Mall. The Gadsden store opened

Isadore Pizitz and his wife, Mickey, smile for the camera during the grand opening ceremonies for the new Pizitz store on Dexter Avenue in downtown Montgomery, 1972. Unfortunately, downtown Montgomery was not quite ready for a major department store, and that Pizitz closed four years later. *Author's collection.*

COME ON IN, OUR '73
SWIMWEAR SELECTION'S FINE!

Come see the fashion excitement our new swimwear from Catalina and "In" is causing! Come take your pick, from bikinis,
sheaths, one-piece or modified two-piece styles, only 2 of which
we show: Catalina's 100% nylon swimdress in pink or sapphire,
sizes 12-18 . . . $28. "In" blue batik "no bra" bikini with wild
peekaboo cutout sides! 100% Antron® nylon, 5 to 13 . . . . . $17.
Come on in, see 'em all!

sportswear and junior sportswear, third floor, and all suburban stores

As we have seen already, Pizitz's newspaper ads featured a wide variety of artwork styles. These beach bunnies promoted Catalina swimwear during the summer of 1973; we aren't sure what ladies were supposed to do who weren't quite this stick-thin. *Jo Lawley collection.*

in the new mall on U.S. Highway 11 in 1974; unlike most of the Pizitz mall stores, it occupied only one level. In an interview at the time, Richard Pizitz stated that this would be the first complete department store to be built in Gadsden.

The Pizitz at Brookwood Village opened on July 31, 1975. It consisted of 104,000 square feet of retail space—bigger than either the Eastwood Mall or Five Points West branches—and the newspapers made much of its main feature: a two-story "open well" in the center of the store, where the escalators and departments for silver and fine gifts were located. (Although the building has since served as a McRae's, Parisian and is currently a Belk store, this center well has remained unchanged.) Still trusting in the need for department stores to live up to their name, the Brookwood Pizitz had fashions on the upper level, while the bottom level was an eclectic mix of furniture, housewares, sporting goods, televisions, appliances, toys, candy, books and records, a beauty shop, a travel agency, an optical department and, of course, yet another Pizitz Bake Shop.

The era of the "big box" retailer was coming, but in 1975 it could still barely be glimpsed on the horizon.

Even further down the road, geographically and timewise, a location in Florence opened in August 1978. It was the tenth in the chain but was less than half the size of the previous mall stores, at forty thousand square feet, and concentrated primarily on fashions. That same month, a "junior version" of a Pizitz store (twelve thousand square feet), designated a Budget Store, opened in West Lake Mall in Bessemer, replacing the first branch store that had opened in 1956. Like the Florence store, this one would be devoted to

When Birmingham's Brookwood Village mall opened in 1975, Pizitz was one of the original anchor stores. Here we see the building under construction and Isadore, Richard, Michael and Merritt Pizitz studying the floor plan in preparation for the grand opening. *Dixie Neon and Pizitz family collections.*

apparel, without any of the additional amenities except a beauty salon. Pizitz had long ago passed old rival Loveman's in number of stores, as Loveman's had peaked at four locations in Birmingham, plus one in Huntsville and one in Montgomery.

With the number of stores in the chain growing at such a pace, it was a particularly difficult pill to take when one of them went out of business—the only Pizitz store to have done so at the time. The downtown Montgomery outlet had never performed as well as expected, and early in 1976, the family took it off life support. In the official company newsletter, Richard Pizitz spoke frankly about what happened:

> *Simply put, downtown Montgomery cannot support a major department store. Had we built a much smaller store, we would undoubtedly have kept it open. But sheer size of the store was such that we were losing money.*

We thought that downtown Montgomery was going to make a comeback because of the major urban renewal efforts that were being made there. We looked at Montgomery and said, "Here is one of the largest cities in the South that does not have a downtown department store." We thought with the state capitol being only six blocks away and with the great number of employees there, this might be a long-term opportunity.

DARTH VADER—
IN PERSON
Pizitz

The original Darth Vader
lives on!
The menacing 6 ft. 8 in.
star of Star Wars.
See him in person,
get his autograph!

tomorrow, Thursday
Downtown 11 am till 12
Eastwood 3 pm till 4
5 Pts. West 7 pm till 8

Friday
Roebuck 11 am till 12
Brookwood 3 pm till 4

STAR WARS™

Liberty Star Wars jeans and overalls
for boys and girls

Jeans and overalls of easy care
Celanese Fortrel® polyester and cotton
with an all over Star Wars print.
Jeans, sizes 2 to 7 5.50
Overalls, sizes 2 to 7 11.80
Star Wars knit shirts
Short sleeves, sizes 4-7 $4
children's world, all Pizitz stores
Fortrel® is a registered trademark of Fiber Industries Inc.,
a subsidiary of Celanese Corp.

It is hard to say what is more disturbing about this December 1978 ad: the concept of Darth Vader signing autographs for the kiddies at Pizitz or the idea of Liberty Trousers manufacturing *Star Wars*–themed denim jeans and overalls. *Author's collection.*

Richard and his brothers—not to mention dad Isadore, who was by no means counted out of the process yet—were determined to not let Montgomery be a spot on their escutcheon. Even as plans got underway to convert the former downtown store into an office building, the announcement was made that a new Pizitz would open in Montgomery's Eastdale Mall in October 1977. Its grand opening ceremony was preceded by a rather unusual ad campaign: the two words "Take Flight" and a drawing of a hot air balloon on yellow and blue metal shirt tags that were circulated around Montgomery for weeks. For the actual opening day, balloonist Robert Suit was scheduled to make a flight over Montgomery in his seven-story balloon, with a huge Pizitz banner trailing in his wake.

Back home in downtown Birmingham, Pizitz tried

something new for Easter 1976. For many years, Loveman's had used a "Breakfast with Santa" program as its ammunition in the Yuletide retail war, so Pizitz countered with "Breakfast with the Easter Bunny." The launch of this promotion caused some old-time employees to fondly remember the long-ago annual egg hunts at Avondale Park, but even they had to admit that an indoor event such as the breakfast was less susceptible to Alabama's unpredictable springtime weather. There is no record of whether Kurt Hertrich provided carrot cake for the big bunny's dessert.

(With Pizitz's long-established Easter traditions, it is somewhat surprising that the store never attempted to transform the sixth-floor auditorium into a bunny-themed parallel to the Enchanted Forest. Proving the room's flexibility, almost immediately after the 1976 forest was dismantled, the auditorium became a temporary "Circus Land" exhibit to tie in with the Ringling Brothers/Barnum and Bailey aggregation's annual appearance in Birmingham. Instead of elves and reindeer, the auditorium was filled with a collection of vintage costumes and posters from the Circus World Museum of Baraboo, Wisconsin.)

You know it has to be the late 1970s when Pizitz's massive display windows were carrying the theme "DISCO...Anything Goes!" *Sylvia Martin collection.*

The 1970s saw Pizitz developing several memorable advertising campaigns. Up to that time, the daily newspaper ads had been the store's main outlet for promotion. Staff artists Eugenia Ashworth, Virginia Garrard, Lucille Thomas and Dorothy Haas turned out stunning artwork for ad after ad, most of which would be seen by the public only once.

The newspaper ads were supplemented by occasional television commercials, but until the late 1960s or early 1970s, there was no overall theme or slogan for them. For example, one commercial that ran during the 1972 Christmas season featured beautifully photographed slides of scenes in the Enchanted Forest, which dissolved into one another as a lullaby-like holiday song played in the background: "Christmas, children enchanted / Snowflakes and reindeer / Santa is here now…" One of the earliest coordinated television and radio ad campaigns, dating from roughly the same period, was built around the slogan "Put a Little Pizitz in Your Life." That one was the brainchild of ad man Dick Morrison, who had slick commercials filmed in Nashville. Besides the usual broadcast exposure, Pizitz took the unusual step of having the commercials edited into sixty-second spots that ran before the main feature in Birmingham movie theaters. Only the high quality of their production could have kept them from looking as cheesy as a rat's refrigerator when enlarged on the silver screen.

Around 1972, Morrison headed up a committee to develop one of the store's most unusual radio/television/print campaigns. It faced head on the most challenging

Pizitz's annual Christmas catalogue always had stunning photography on its cover. These examples, clockwise from top left, are from 1972, 1976, 1978 and 1979. *Pizitz family collection.*

Right: Pizitz employed several different slogans for its advertising during the latter half of the 1970s, but one of the most enduring was "You've Got Style…I've Got Pizitz," as seen in this Easter-themed newspaper ad. *Brittain Phillips collection.*

Below: The strikingly beautiful model Jerri Jordan delivered the "I've Got Pizitz" line in ad after ad during the 1980s. *Jess Bullock collection.*

aspect of promoting the Pizitz stores—namely, the fact that people who had not always lived in Birmingham had absolutely no idea how to pronounce Pizitz when they saw it in print and had even less of an idea how to spell it when they heard it pronounced on radio or TV. (To this day, the students at Pizitz Middle School face the same problem whenever they have dealings with other educational institutions.) Rather than fighting it, Morrison's new campaign was built around the blunt slogan "What's a Pizitz?"

This theme opened up an entire world of humorous ads, each of which incorporated some phrase that could be confused with the Pizitz name. Some of the "answers" to "What's a Pizitz?" included "Isn't that some leaning tower in Italy?" ("Sorry, chum, that's Pisa!"), "Isn't it a crisp, round cracker?" ("Ritz'll love you, lover!"), "Isn't she that gorgeous opera singer?" ("No, dumdum, that's Marguerite Piazza!"), "Isn't he that famous way-out artist?" ("Well, it ain't Picasso, but it's famous and near in!"), "Isn't that like, you know, jazzy?" ("You mean pizzazz, kiddo!") and so on.

The ad campaign for the 1977 Christmas season prominently featured members of the Birmingham Ballet. The newspaper ads were topped with the logo of a ballerina unwrapping a giant package, and the scene was played out by live ballerinas in the television commercials. These were among the first of Pizitz's commercials produced by Jess Bullock and his advertising agency, and as we will see in our next chapter, during the ensuing years he would be responsible for using television to once again remake the Pizitz image.

With ten stores in the chain, Pizitz seemed to be ending the 1970s as undisputed king of the Birmingham retail jungle. That would prove to be even truer soon after the 1980s got underway—but no one could have foreseen that Pizitz would not survive the end of another decade.

Chapter 7

THERE'S A PIZITZ
AT PIZITZ

P eople had barely gotten used to writing 1980 on their checks, instead of 1979, when one of the biggest bombshells in Birmingham's retailing history was dropped. During the first week of April, and with only a few days' notice, Loveman's abruptly went out of business.

The underlying reasons for this really had little to do with Loveman's performance, although it is true that the market for its type of full-line department stores was slowly drying up. Loveman's main troubles lay with its parent company, City Stores of New York, which had been its owner since 1927. City Stores, with a number of chains throughout the country, declared bankruptcy and sold off as many of its holdings as possible to new owners. Loveman's was not one of the lucky ones, so four of its six stores closed forever.

What about the other two? That is where Louis Pizitz was no doubt chortling from his grave. The Loveman's stores at Western Hills Mall and Century Plaza were bought by Pizitz and would reopen under that rival's name two weeks after Loveman's bit the dust. Pizitz, of course, had no interest in the downtown Loveman's building since it had its own seven-story monolith to worry about, and it also needed no further stores in the areas where Loveman's other branches operated (West Lake Mall in Bessemer, plus one store each in Huntsville and Montgomery). Actually, there was already a bit of double coverage in that the Century Plaza Loveman's was catty-cornered across U.S. Highway 78 from the Pizitz at Eastwood Mall. Pizitz wasted no time in announcing that the Eastwood store would close

This was the "missy dresses" display in the third-floor women's fashions department in 1980. Even though the era of the downtown department store was drawing to a close, Pizitz never let the quality or variety of its visual merchandising suffer. *Earle Cappellen collection.*

in order to move operations over to Century Plaza. (Those who are prone to keep up with such data will recall that eventually Service Merchandise moved into the former Eastwood Mall Pizitz building.)

Although to the casual observer there would have seemed to be little or no difference in the mall Pizitz and Loveman's stores, underneath the surface the two chains actually did take differing approaches to their merchandising and display efforts. While the former Loveman's stores were closed, Pizitz set about changing out the contents to fit the chain's own established format. Remodeling to conform to the Pizitz image would take a bit longer. Charles Elliott, as part of Jim Luker's staff, was given the responsibility of redecorating the Western Hills and Century Plaza locations. He says that Western Hills in particular needed some emergency cosmetic surgery. Loveman's had decorated that store in a shocking color combination of orange, lime green and hot pink that would have looked right at home in a bowl of Trix cereal; over the next few months, Elliott would do his best to subdue the color scheme to match Pizitz's personality.

After acquiring two of Loveman's former locations, Pizitz kept expanding in the early 1980s. A location finally opened in Tuscaloosa's MacFarland Mall later in 1980, initially overlapping with that mall's location in the Sam Pizitz chain. In fact, the Tuscaloosa Pizitzes initially tried to block the Birmingham Pizitzes from muscling in on their territory, and the dispute had

Since 1925, Pizitz's corner window had been the prime location for the largest and most elaborate displays. This one from the early 1980s was typical, with its combination of scenery, props and the ever-present mannequins in lifelike poses. *Sylvia Martin collection.*

to be settled in court. The judgment was that both stores could operate in the mall, one as Pizitz and the other as "Pizitz of Birmingham." It all turned out to be a moot point, since the Sam Pizitz chain went out of business the next year. A second Huntsville store was brought to Madison Square Mall in 1984.

The Pizitz Bake Shops were still cooking up healthy profits under Kurt Hertrich's watchful eye—or they were until the recession of 1980 hit. Suddenly, the price of sugar skyrocketed, and even the most novice cook could tell that that commodity was the primary ingredient in anything sold in the bake shops. When profits began falling faster than a cake in the oven, in 1982 Hertrich got out while the getting was good, going into business for himself by opening the Swiss Pastry Shop and, later, a company known simply as Wedding Cakes by Kurt. The Pizitz Bake Shops limped along without him for a while, but the spirit just was not there anymore. Besides, those outlets were facing increased competition from ever-more-convenient bake shops in every supermarket, particularly the largest ones such as Food World. During 1983 and 1984, the Pizitz Bake Shops in Decatur, Ensley, Montgomery's Eastgate Mall and even the counter in the downtown skywalk had been closed.

In 1982, *Birmingham* magazine sent writer Dale Short to ferret out the Pizitz success story, which it published in December of that year under the heading "Department Store Dynasty." Isadore made himself available for the interview, but most of the talking was done by the new generation, as represented by Richard, Michael and Merritt. Each of the three brothers had his own point of view on the challenges of keeping a department store in tune with changing times, but Richard perhaps gave the most succinct summary: "We have to keep in mind not only who our customers are today, but who they'll be five years from now, ten years from now. You have to look at birth cycles, age-group growth, demographics. With the growth of single households, for instance, with people marrying and having children much later in life, we're seeing a totally different set of needs and tastes."

Merritt put a definite early 1980s spin on the same topic: "Sometimes the demand for a certain product will barely exist and then, BAM!, the market just explodes. It was that way with digital calculators, and more recently with video games. But the same thing is true, to some extent, even with fashion. You've got to be aware a lot quicker than before."

While it might have been sheer coincidence, the demise of Loveman's was quickly followed by a concentrated attempt on Pizitz's part to accelerate its ongoing efforts to reshape its image into that of a more upscale retailer. As we have seen, this trend began in the mid-1960s when Fred Rauschenberg had been charged with getting the stores out of their fuddy-duddy rut. Now, with Jess Bullock and the Bullock Agency in charge of the broadcast advertising, the Pizitz image was going to receive its most extreme makeover yet.

Bullock received instructions from the family that no longer were the television commercials to promote specific merchandise, announcing the

Using the Brookwood Village store as a setting, during the 1980s Richard Pizitz filmed a series of commercials assuring customers that, indeed, "There's a Pizitz at Pizitz." *Jess Bullock collection.*

price for all to hear. Instead, henceforth that would be left to newspaper ads, while the Pizitz commercials concentrated totally on image. The new keyword was to be "style," and Bullock and his staff soon came up with a slogan to carry each and every ad: "You've Got Style...You've Got Pizitz!"

Watching the commercials of the early 1980s today, there is no doubt that they fell firmly into the era of disco and *Dallas*. Most of them were built around the stunning beauty of model Jerri Jordan, who could appear alternately playful, studious, dangerously sensual and any of a dozen other moods that were called for. The jingle the Bullock Agency crafted was set to a pounding beat, and its brief lyrics drove home the fact that this was a new Pizitz:

> *Puttin' on Pizitz (the look)!*
> *Pizitz (the feeling)!*
> *Pizitz! Puttin' on Pizitz!*
> *You, you're looking for the fashion,*
> *You, that certain kind of style (style!),*
> *A touch of flair and magic (magic!),*
> *You've got style...I've got Pizitz!*

As the disco era was packed away with the leisure suits, the "disco jingle" was not getting "style" over as well as it originally did, so a new jingle was composed that built to a rousing climax: "Uniquely, completely, to say it distinctly, you've got style!" "I've got Pizitz!" That one was followed by still a third one with the "style" keyword: "For the times of your life, it's Pizitz and you / For the style of your life, it's Pizitz and you / Going, doing, feeling, living / You've got...style! Pizitz!"

These jingles were played against images filmed anywhere and everywhere in Birmingham and, for one memorable series, even in the Bahamas. (Quite a stretch from when Louis Pizitz sold material for three cents a yard.) Pizitz and the Bullock Agency were fittingly rewarded by winning the top fashion award from the National Merchants' Retail Association (NMRA) four years in a row.

With the downtown Loveman's building silent and empty after forty-five years—not counting the business's long history stretching back before that store was built in 1935—Pizitz was one of the only major retailers left in the former center of activity. In the past, when the downtown store needed to attract more attention, what was the solution? You guessed it, folks—it was time for yet another remodeling program!

This time, Jim Luker was the overseer for the whole project, and in an interview in October 1983, he explained how the store's variety of departments would be reshuffled into what became their final lineup:

> *We are going to bring related departments closer together. For example, on the second floor we have brought toys and all other children's areas together; on the first floor, we have all our men's departments together...prior to that, they were separated, some on second floor and some on first floor; on the third floor we have all of our ready-to-wear departments; on the fourth floor are all of our home furnishings departments; and then on the fifth floor we have managed to bring together all of our "big ticket" items...appliances, TV's, stereos, furniture, carpet, everything.*

You might have noticed from that itemized list that one of the formerly most prominent floors was left out. "This gave us a chance to take a good, hard look at some of our departments that were overspaced," Luker said, "and we realized that we could totally empty our sixth floor by taking these departments and absorbing them into more appropriate locations." As we have already seen, the Enchanted Forest had moved from the auditorium into the corner window the previous Christmas; now there would be no retail on the sixth floor at all. The area that was formerly the auditorium was carved into cubicles to serve as the advertising department. Its two walls of windows, providing both northern and

This handsome photo of the Pizitz family was taken on the main floor of the downtown store while it was decorated for the 1982 Christmas season. *Back, left to right*: Richard Jr., Michael, Richard, Merritt and Jeff; *front*: Nancy Pizitz Nagrodzky and Isadore Pizitz. *Author's collection.*

eastern light, must have seemed like getting out of prison for the advertising artists who had formerly been squirreled away in the upper regions of the 1952 annex building. Luker's display (or visual merchandising) offices were also moved out of the annex, which was then closed and almost forgotten by everyone.

Just because no merchandise departments were on the sixth floor did not mean it was closed off to the public. One of its features, located near the elevators, was the Soul Scissors hair salon. For several years, Pizitz had contracted the operation of its beauty salons, both downtown and in the branch stores, to the New York agency Seligman and Latz. This company was also involved when the store decided to open this specialty salon for African American women. A few years later, Jim Luker reminisced about the outrageous color scheme of this particular department: "Coretta Scott King was working with Seligman and Latz at the time Pizitz decided to provide this service to our customers," he said. "Mrs. King and I met privately for almost an hour, and discussed the location and attitudes changing in the South. I was very impressed with the lady."

Things had changed a lot, without a doubt…and they would continue to change. Reading the promotional literature for Soul Scissors today, with its abundance of 1970s-era slang, makes it sound almost as outdated as some of the racist literature of a much earlier time: "OUTASIGHT! Yes, that's the word for the super-cool, super-beautiful way we work with your hair. Soul Scissors is the one place you can really get it together with a staff of brothers and sisters who want you to be SOMEBODY black! Be what you are, do what you like, and the staff of Soul Scissors gets you where you want to go!" Can somebody say "Right on!"?

During this same period, an unusual series of television spots was produced that featured Richard Pizitz as on-screen host, a role he had not previously played. The point of this particular series of commercials was to assure customers that, despite all the nation's department stores that had been sold and bought by new owners, "There IS a Pizitz at Pizitz." Before long, though, there would be one less executive by that name.

When word came out that Isadore Pizitz had died of cancer at age eighty-one on March 17, 1985, the general public could not have been blamed for wondering what this meant for the future of the stores. Richard, as president of the chain, served as spokesman to the media. About his dad's five-year battle with the disease, Richard said, "He was a man of amazing courage… he continued to come in to work up until 10 days ago."

Pizitz

1821 Second Ave. North
Birmingham, Alabama

HEALTHY HAIR HAPPENS HERE
Black hair is delicate hair, and needs super-care. Making your hair look great is our game. Whether you choose to wear a "Fro" or whether you're into cornrowing or pressing you must start out with healthy hair. Our staff knows all about hair and they'll take the time to rap with you too!

CONDITIONERS ARE OUR THING
And make conditioners your thing too. We use the best conditioners to strengthen your hair and keep its shine. But more than that we give you advice and instructions in at-home care. You want your hair to feel as good as it looks soft and shiny . . . never dry or dull.

SOUL-GRABBING HAIRSTYLES
Never be uptight about your hair. Come in and rap with the brothers and sisters. They dig what you're after. They cut, press, braid and are into everything you need for styles that are right on. Styling that relates to the way you look and the way you live.

BE SOMEBODY BLACK
We say it again. No hang-ups, but black awareness is what we're all after. It's an identity thing to do your "own thing." Come in to Soul Scissors and we'll help you find your look.

SOUL SCISSORS

Subscribing to the concept that it was always best to find a need and fill it, Pizitz established the Soul Scissors hair salon on the sixth floor. While intentions were good, some of the lingo in this brochure sounds a bit outdated today. *Author's collection.*

Friends of the family presented much the same story. Isadore's personal attorney, Karl B. Friedman, said, "I was visiting with him last Thursday. He knew he was dying. He was not concerned about himself; more than anything else, he wanted his sons to continue to be happy together in their business and family relationships."

The death of Isadore was the first sign that the winds of change were about to start blowing through downtown's canyons once more. He had been the living link to his famous father, having been with the store since the first portion of the downtown building was constructed, and now he would no longer be around to remind everyone of how things used to be. Richard, Michael and Merritt, however, were determined to keep the family business going, and during 1986 two more stores were opened: one in Hoover's enormous new Riverchase Galleria and one near the Florida state line in Dothan.

A June 1986 newspaper feature on the Pizitz family rather graphically illustrated how the nature of department stores was changing, even more than the *Birmingham* magazine article four years earlier. The middle-class shopper who once went to Pizitz to buy clothing, appliances and toys was more and more gravitating toward all-purpose retailers such as Wal-Mart, which had the same departments but in a much less elegant setting. The reporter noted, "Pizitz has shifted its focus to selling goods that are more fashionable, better quality and higher priced than before."

Michael gave an example: "Five years ago, shoppers might have bought a half ounce of Faberge or Jovan perfume for $20 to $25. Now they will find no Faberge or Jovan; instead, that half ounce bottle will be Estee Lauder or Calvin Klein, at $60 to $90." Richard chimed in, "The goal has been to become a store that is a fashion leader, a store that aims at people with updated tastes, but a store that sticks to the original precepts of my grandfather, which were quality and value." Michael pointed out that Pizitz's private, hometown ownership might have been a major reason it survived when Loveman's did not. At that, questioned whether the Pizitz family would ever consider selling out to a larger chain, Richard's answer was an unqualified no. In fact, he revealed plans for Pizitz to move into some adjoining states, specifically Georgia, Tennessee and Mississippi, with a goal of opening a new store in those locations every year and a half.

Well, as the saying goes, that was then. Not long after that article ran, the Pizitz brothers were approached by representatives of another—and, yes, larger—southern department store chain. Jackson, Mississippi's McRae's stores were almost as old as Pizitz, having been founded in 1902 by Samuel P. McRae. Like Pizitz, McRae's was still a family operation, with Samuel's son Richard as chairman of the board and Richard Jr. as president of the company. McRae's had been licking its chops for some time in anticipation of moving into the Alabama market. It had one store in Mobile, but its fifteen other outlets were scattered over its home state, with a pair of additional ones in the Florida panhandle and an isolated one in Monroe, Louisiana. McRae's desperately wanted the thirteen Pizitz stores, and it did not care how much it had to pay to obtain them.

Like the sudden demise of Loveman's, the announcement that Pizitz's end was near came with little advance warning. On December 10, 1986, the news broke that McRae's would be taking over Pizitz on the last day of the year. Richard Pizitz assured loyal customers that there should be little noticeable difference once the sale took place. McRae's had not decided whether to change the name on the stores, he said, so for the time being they would remain branded as Pizitz. Inasmuch as Pizitz was a privately held company, he would go into no more details about just how much money McRae's was paying for the chain—but everyone knew it had to be an almost unimaginable sum if it meant the Pizitzes were giving up the family institution. What was on record was that after its purchase of Pizitz, McRae's would be one of the nation's largest privately held department store chains, with twenty-nine locations and annual sales of more than $300 million.

The Pizitz family was not totally happy with the way the sale was being reported in the press. On December 12, Richard sent out a memo to each and every employee, enumerating some of the more egregious errors:

> *Amazingly, the Post-Herald stated that, "Despite two years of record sales, the chain was in trouble." This shoddy and inept reporting is inexcusable. The past two years have been the best in Pizitz history from both a sales and profit standpoint, and while final results for 1986 will not be known for several months, this year will again show record sales and profitable operations.*
>
> *Channel 6 News reported that "only persons with 10 years seniority are guaranteed a job." This is totally false. The Birmingham News commented that "most of the top executives of Pizitz have agreed to step down after a transition period." I have no idea where they came to this conclusion, as this would only relate to my brothers and me. For the most part, the media have reported the Pizitz/McRae story positively; but it was important that you not be misled by some of the inaccuracies that did appear.*
>
> *I would like to thank so many Pizitz associates for the kind and thoughtful words expressed to my brothers and me this week. We value your friendship, your loyalty, and I know that Pizitz associates will continue to give their best efforts in the future.*

And so it came to pass: as of January 1, 1987, the Pizitz family no longer owned Pizitz. As had been hinted in the December 12 memo, Richard, Michael and Merritt were not part of the new McRae's version of their company, but Michael's son Jeff and Richard's son Richard Jr. did stay on to help ease things through the transition period. Jim Luker also remained to handle whatever display direction McRae's might choose to pursue in its new Alabama locations.

The three Pizitz brothers were not completely out of the retail business, though. Back in the mid-1970s, the Pizitz family had acquired the Birmingham and Nashville franchises for high-end clothing store Gus Mayer, which they would retain and operate as a separate company. They also had their hands in several Great American Cookie Company stores (apparently being completely unwilling to let go of the Pizitz Bake Shops idea!) and a franchise for the Lynn's Hallmark card shops. Significantly and tellingly, all of these subsidiary businesses operated in malls.

Epilogue

THE NOT-SO-BUSY
CORNER

While the initial articles about the sale of Pizitz had included the comforting thought that McRae's had not decided what to do about changing the name on the stores, most people realized that was just a case of whistling past the old retailers' graveyard. By the summer of 1987, newspaper ads were carrying both logos, in their completely different type styles, giving the name as a hybridized "McRae's/Pizitz." At the same time, the Pizitz name on the directional signs around the Riverchase Galleria had already been changed to McRae's. The stated goal was to have all Pizitz signage replaced by the McRae's logo by mid-September.

"Although Pizitz has a wonderful name in the Birmingham community," Richard McRae Jr. told the *Birmingham News*, "we felt it was important to make the change for reasons of economies of scale. We have a McRae's in Meridian, Mississippi and a Pizitz in Tuscaloosa, and we saw an overlap of markets there. We had to advertise as Pizitz in one town and McRae's in the other. The same is true in the Florence area with Tupelo. It is just much simpler to have one name." And, of course, it was obvious that McRae's was not going to change its name to Pizitz.

One of the buildings with two exterior signs—although they were nowhere as large as that of their predecessor—was the downtown store. It seemed curious that McRae's would continue to operate what had amounted to a brontosaurus on Nineteenth Street, but tradition held out for a short while. Extinction was not far away, though. On February 2, 1988, a year and two months after buying Pizitz, McRae's made the formal announcement

After McRae's bought the Pizitz chain at the end of 1986, it waited approximately six months before retiring the famous Birmingham name. Here, a crew replaces the Pizitz signage on the Riverchase Galleria store with the McRae's logo. *Birmingham Public Library collection.*

that the downtown store would be closed. Richard McRae was once again forced to defend his actions to the Birmingham populace: "At the time of our purchase of Pizitz, we had every intention of continuing to operate a department store in downtown Birmingham. Merchandise assortments were expanded, presentation was improved, and we increased our advertising." It was all for naught, he explained, as the downtown store failed to rise above 2 percent of McRae's total sales.

Two days before the closing, the newspaper ran a story that was, in effect, an obituary. "Store windows along 19th Street at McRae's downtown location, which only a few weeks ago were beautifully decorated with inviting Christmas displays, already have given way to blackened windows filled only with signs to let people know that a clearance sale is in progress," it sighed.

Customers and former employees took the opportunity to reminisce about the building's long history. Mr. and Mrs. Lou McCracken were shopping in the basement when a newspaper reporter caught up with them. Lou was glad to point out the area where his wife worked in the shoe department, and Mrs. McCracken poured out the details: "I used to work after school and on Saturday nights during the war years. Back then, you had to have ration stamps for shoes. But we had some shoes for which you didn't have to have rations, and we put those on a table. For 75 cents a pair, you could get platform shoes, high heels and colors."

One shopper put it in the simplest terms: "I hate to see the old lady go."

Once the doors to the downtown store were locked on Saturday, February 27, there was not much left to say. Jim Luker moved his display office from

For a brief time, McRae's ran newspaper ads that contained both logos, but by the fall of 1987, the Pizitz name had been erased for good. *Author's collection.*

the sixth floor to the Brookwood Village location but retired in February 1989. Even without his help, the McRae's stores continued to thrive—so much so that they eventually faced the same fate as Pizitz. In 1995, McRae's was acquired by Tennessee's Proffitt's department stores, which were in turn swallowed by the giant Belk chain of North Carolina a decade later. The McRae's brand name ceased to exist in March 2006.

During the 1990s, any mention of the Pizitz stores was simply a matter of occasional nostalgia. In May 1991, *Birmingham News* writer Tom Gordon crafted an in-depth article about downtown's former role as the hub of activity. The article, naturally, concentrated mostly on Pizitz and Loveman's; there were striking differences in the descriptions of the condition of the two former stores' interiors, owing to the fact that Pizitz had been empty for only three years while Loveman's had been abandoned for more than a decade. Accompanying Richard Pizitz into the old building, writer Gordon noted that near one of the doorways sat "a jumble of mementos from the store's long past, quietly awaiting the Pizitz family's decision on what to do with them." Apparently that decision-making process dragged on for too long, because that collection of historic artifacts disappeared shortly thereafter.

One of the now missing pieces described in the article was a framed painting that had been done for the cover of a Pizitz Christmas catalogue. It was said to depict the exterior of the store during the holiday season, although whether it included the giant corner tree was not specified. Richard

Pizitz's comment upon seeing it again was, "There haven't been that many people on the sidewalk in the last ten years combined." Like the rest of the memorabilia pile, the Christmas painting has yet to resurface anywhere.

Memories of Christmas at Pizitz made the news again a year and a half later. Since leaving the display department in 1983, former Enchanted Forest associate Charles Elliott had spent time in the service of various other Birmingham stores and, by the 1992 Christmas season, had landed at the downtown Bromberg's Jewelers. At the encouragement of Operation New Birmingham, Bromberg's decided to revive the tradition of animated windows and charged Elliott with recreating his work for Pizitz.

Elliott did not reach back to the ill-fated 1981 attempt to create an Enchanted Forest of the future, but he did manage to rent a few of the former Pizitz figures from Ed's Pet World, and the Bromberg's window on Second Avenue was soon drawing attention just as the original downtown windows had done. Most amazingly, people could be seen standing on the sidewalk and gazing at the window at 11:00 p.m. on a Sunday, something that no other remaining retail store downtown had been able to manage. The experiment was repeated for the 1993 Christmas season but after that was allowed to once again fade into memory.

While the former Loveman's building found a new life as the McWane Science Center, the Pizitz building (no one ever referred to it as the McRae's building, even though that was the name on it when it closed) continued to deteriorate. Occasional vagrants would somehow find their way inside, but otherwise it remained basically the same as the day it closed. The merchandise and most of the fixtures were gone, but the carpet on the floor

When Bayer Properties first acquired the downtown Pizitz building in 2000, it hosted an open house for former employees to visit and reminisce about their association with the store. *Author's collection.*

still designated where the aisles used to be, and each of the levels retained remnants of that last grand 1983 remodeling program.

The sixth floor showed no evidence of its career as a source of Christmas wonderment, although the telltale post that had once marked the center of the Enchanted Forest could still be located among all the abandoned advertising cubicles. (Since McRae's had its own advertising staff in the Mississippi home office, those who had toiled over Pizitz's print ads were let go soon after the buyout.) Even almost thirty years after the store was closed, an office door on the sixth floor continued to bear the nameplate of the nonexistent Dolly Dale.

On the fifth floor, in the suite of offices that once belonged to Louis and his descendants, boxes and boxes of store files still sat awaiting their final fate. As time dragged by, the aforementioned vagrants would occasionally have need of a box and would unceremoniously dump the contents onto the floor. Reams of store papers and mail-order catalogues were strewn about like so much garbage. Curiously, whatever existed as a photo archive had disappeared and, to date, has still never been located.

Developer Bayer Properties acquired the building and, in October 2000, announced that it would be reopened for two days to hold a reunion of past employees and customers. Video cameras were set up, and attendees were encouraged to share their memories in oral histories. The stated goal was that the interviews would be incorporated into a documentary about the downtown theater and retail district—but the proposed film was never produced, and like the photo archives, the interviews have never been seen again.

After that event, very few people got to see the inside of the building. Just seeing the outside was bad enough, as most of the windows were broken out by either vandals (on the lower levels) or harsh weather (on the upper levels). Finally, in early 2010, Bayer Properties announced that it was going forward with its plans to redevelop the building as office space on the upper six floors and a combination of retail and restaurants on the street floor.

This news attracted much favorable media coverage, even though the first phases of Pizitz's new life were not due to be finished until 2012. At about the same time this project was to begin, the Pizitz family announced that they would be moving their Gus Mayer store out of the Brookwood Village mall—where it had been since 1975—and into the more upscale Summit shopping development. Retail had continued to evolve even after the closing of the downtown Pizitz store and renaming of the other outlets in the chain; malls, which had been largely responsible for putting downtown shopping out of business, had bloomed and died and by the 2010s were as obsolete as their retail predecessors of the 1920s and 1930s. The trend had shifted back to shopping centers where people could park near the entrance to their favorite store rather than tramping through mall corridors to get there. Richard Pizitz Jr. kept up his father's tradition as family spokesman by noting, "We listen to our customers and try to monitor our customers' shopping habits. More and more of them are shopping at the Summit, and we need to follow our customers instead of our customers following us." The Pizitzes also announced their launch of a new business venture, a chain of frozen yogurt shops to be known simply as "32°," with Bayer Properties helping find appropriate shopping center outlets throughout the Southeast.

Meanwhile, back at the crumbling old downtown building, the different nature of an office building from a retail store meant that some of Pizitz's

This and next two pages: These four views show how the Pizitz building looked as Bayer Properties began its renovation into a combination retail/office complex in early 2010. *Above*: The once grand main floor and original Westinghouse escalators; *page 119, top*: the former sixth-floor auditorium, looking definitely deforested and not so enchanting; *page 119, bottom*: the former yummy-smelling bakery counter site on the skywalk from the parking deck into the third floor...the only smells there now are mold and mildew; *page 120*: the restaurant on the mezzanine, where the booths still await customers who will never come again. *Author's collection.*

traditional elements were going to need to be radically changed. The elevator shafts, for example, were to be moved to the center of the building rather than rising along its southern wall. The 1965 skywalk had been neglected so badly in the intervening years that it was structurally unsound and would have to be rebuilt in order for the office building to utilize the parking deck. The same went for the annex, the former Store for Men, which was deemed too dangerous to even enter.

And so, more than 110 years after Louis Pizitz acted on his wife's whim and deserted Georgia for Birmingham, the store he built seemed to have a life after all. What would he have thought about his carefully planned building being drastically altered to suit twenty-first-century needs? No one can say for sure, but inasmuch as he was never loath to undertake a new remodeling program during his own lifetime, not to mention the many times his son and grandsons did the same, it is probably safe to say that he would just be comfortable knowing that the building was going to continue to serve a useful purpose.

Maybe, just maybe, once offices are occupying Pizitz, late-night workers might hear the occasional faint ringing of a cash register or the distinctive "ding" of the long-gone elevators. Up on the sixth floor, they might notice the distant sound of Christmas music and a hearty "ho ho ho" at certain times of the year. And if they look very closely, they may catch a glimpse of an elderly man sitting in a chair on the third floor, watching over them as if they are "his children."

BIBLIOGRAPHY

BOOKS

Atkins, Leah Rawls. *The Valley and the Hills: An Illustrated History of Birmingham and Jefferson County.* Woodland Hills, CA: Windsor Publications, 1981.

Bird, William L., Jr. *Holidays on Display.* New York: Princeton Architectural Press, 2007.

Century Plus: A Bicentennial Portrait of Birmingham, Alabama. Birmingham, AL: Oxmoor Press, 1976.

Hollis, Tim. *Birmingham Broadcasting.* Charleston, SC: Arcadia Publishing, 2006.

———. *Birmingham's Theater and Retail District.* Charleston, SC: Arcadia Publishing, 2005.

———. *Christmas Wishes: A Catalog of Vintage Holiday Treats and Treasures.* Mechanicsburg, PA: Stackpole Books, 2010.

———. *Vintage Birmingham Signs.* Charleston, SC: Arcadia Publishing, 2007.

King, Pamela Sterne. *50 Years and Counting: A History of Operation New Birmingham.* Birmingham, AL: Operation New Birmingham, 2008.

Lifson, Hal. *1966: A Personal View of the Coolest Year in Pop Culture History.* Chicago: Bonus Books, 2002.

Marling, Karal Ann. *Merry Christmas! Celebrating America's Greatest Holiday.* Cambridge, MA: Harvard University Press, 2000.

McMillan, Malcolm C. *Yesterday's Birmingham.* Miami, FL: E.A. Seemann Publishing, 1975.

O'Donnell, Joe. *The Forge: Metal to Medicine.* Birmingham, AL: Regional Chamber of Commerce, 2007.

Portrait of Birmingham. Birmingham, AL: Birmingham Centennial Corporation, 1971.

White, Marjorie Longenecker. *Downtown Birmingham.* Birmingham, AL: Birmingham Historical Society, 1977.

Whiting, Marvin. *Vestavia Hills, Alabama: A Place Apart.* Birmingham, AL: Vestavia Hills Historical Society, 2000.

NEWSPAPER AND MAGAZINE ARTICLES

Aldridge, Jane. "Pizitz will leaves store control to son." *Birmingham News*, July 16, 1959.

Beiman, Irving. "Pizitz' new 7-deck parking facility opens." *Birmingham News*, December 15, 1965.

———. "Pizitz opens new store in West Lake Mall." *Birmingham News*, August 4, 1978.

———. "Pizitz to build at Roebuck Plaza." *Birmingham News*, September 20, 1959.

———. "Pizitz to open remodeled fifth floor." *Birmingham News*, November 20, 1966.

———. "Pizitz to spend million to remodel." *Birmingham News*, April 19, 1959.

———. "$6 million outlay planned in Pizitz 5 Points store." *Birmingham News*, September 3, 1967.

———. "Whether it's 'Dad' or 'Uncle Louie' Pizitz, he's really 'Mr. Birmingham.'" *Birmingham News*, January 2, 1949.

Birmingham Age-Herald. "Dinner planned for needy here," November 13, 1930.

———. "Pack once held pioneer's whole stock in trade," October 30, 1925.

———. "Poor to be fed on Thanksgiving," November 26, 1929.

Birmingham News. "Dazzling Pizitz-West to open," August 21, 1968.

———. "Eastwood Pizitz will be replaced?" April 14, 1980.

———. Editorial. "Louis Pizitz," June 23, 1959.

———. "Electric news sign on Pizitz is exclusive in state," November 29, 1946.

———. "Fashion leadership image of new Pizitz store," July 30, 1975.

———. "Florence Pizitz opens Wednesday," August 13, 1978.

———. "Louis Pizitz passes after long illness," June 22, 1959.

———. "National award going to display man at Pizitz," December 6, 1973.

———. "New department store will open in Bessemer," September 16, 1956.

———. "Overheated motor sets Pizitz toy display afire," November 27, 1959.

———. "Pizitz acquires Goold Shop," December 31, 1950.

———. "Pizitz announces store to return to Montgomery," November 7, 1976.

———. "Pizitz Easter Bunny here to delight tots," March 19, 1949.

———. "Pizitz formally opens its new Bessemer store," September 17, 1956.

———. "Pizitz Men Store opens its doors," February 8, 1952.

———. "Pizitz store installs moving stairways," November 24, 1947.

———. "Pizitz will serve dinners to needy," November 15, 1931.

———. "Pizitz will spend $100,000 on new elevator system," November 29, 1964.

———. "Snoopy and Pizitz to welcome AEA," February 22, 1970.

———. "30,000 young faces jam downtown district to see Hopalong Cassidy in flesh," September 8, 1951.

———. "Thousands feast at store in city," November 27, 1930.

———. "Thursday is big day for Pizitz-Eastwood," August 17, 1966.

Birmingham Post. "5,000 dinners given for poor," November 25, 1932.

Birmingham Post-Herald. "Completely remodeled first floor will be opened by Pizitz today," April 25, 1960.

———. "Pizitz at Tuscaloosa bought by Jemison," August 20, 1953.

———. "Pizitz plans $2.5 million store in Gadsden Mall," April 4, 1972.

———. "Pizitz to build parking complex," November 23, 1964.

Brown, Donald A. "An All-America Thank You, Mr. Pizitz." *Birmingham* magazine, March 1971.

Caldwell, Lily Mae. "Action at Alamo tame as compared to Davy Crockett's arrival here." *Birmingham News,* June 1, 1955.

Carter, Lane. "Silvia Pizitz comes home for lecture on art tonight." *Birmingham News,* June 4, 1970.

Dean, Charles J. "Pizitz sights, glories persist in memories." *Birmingham News,* October 8, 2000.

Etheridge, Elaine, and Howard Shatz. "Isadore Pizitz, store chairman, dies at age 81." *Birmingham News,* March 18, 1985.

Gordon, Tom. "Remembering downtown." *Birmingham News,* May 12, 1991.

Hargrove, Thomas. "Two Loveman's stores at malls sold to Pizitz." *Birmingham Post-Herald*, April 12, 1980.

Holmes, Ralph. "Pizitz building being converted into offices." *Birmingham News*, April 4, 1976.

Ingram, Charlie. "McRae's plans to close downtown store." *Birmingham News*, February 2, 1988.

Jones, Emily. "Pizitz will open two ex-Loveman stores Friday." *Birmingham News*, April 15, 1980.

Kemp, Kathy. "Downtown, everything's waiting for you." *Birmingham News*, October 8, 2000.

Kent, Dawn. "Gus Mayer is set for Summit move." *Birmingham News*, April 11, 2010.

———. "Yogurt bars set to open in July." *Birmingham News*, June 17, 2010.

Kindred, Ingrid. "Bromberg's, others relight downtown Christmas sparkle." *Birmingham News*, November 28, 1992.

———. "I hate to see the old lady go." *Birmingham News*, February 25, 1988.

Kroman, Edna. "Story of Pizitz parallels that of development of Birmingham." *Birmingham News*, June 3, 1936.

Mendelson, Mitch. "With flour, cocoa, butter, pastry chef creates 'sins.'" *Birmingham Post-Herald*, August 26, 1983.

Meridian [Mississippi] *Star*. "McRae's Stores to purchase Pizitz, Inc.," December 11, 1986.

Montgomery Advertiser. "Pizitz opening set Thursday in Eastdale Mall," October 12, 1977.

"Pizitz of Bessemer to build modern new store." Undated clipping in Birmingham Public Library collection.

"Pizitz to open Huntsville store." Unidentified clipping in Birmingham Public Library collection.

Shatz, Howard. "Building on success, Pizitz executives plan to expand 12-store chain to nearby states." *Birmingham News*, June 9, 1986.

———. "Pizitz family no longer will find their home in their stores." *Birmingham News*, December 11, 1986.

———. "Pizitz to sell retail store chain." *Birmingham News*, December 10, 1986.

Short, Dale. "Department Store Dynasty." *Birmingham* magazine, December 1982.

Sikora, Frank. "Pizitz celebrates completion of thorough modernization." *Birmingham News*, November 20, 1967.

Tomberlin, Michael. "Half of Pizitz project leased." *Birmingham News*, February 7, 2010.

————. "Pizitz building set to start makeover." *Birmingham News*, January 29, 2010.

————. "Pizitz-era memories heading for posterity." *Birmingham News*, September 24, 2000.

Tuscaloosa News. "Sam Pizitz dies; was city merchant," December 28, 1982.

Williams, Roy L. "Lofty plans for Pizitz site." *Birmingham News*, October 8, 2002.

————. "Pizitz brothers carve niche." *Birmingham News*, January 28, 2001.

About the Author

Tim Hollis has been a pop culture historian literally all his life. He likes to tell how, when he was nine years old, he was writing letters to companies and trying to preserve the memories of things from when he was three years old. This unhealthy obsession with living in the past has resulted in seventeen books, ranging in subjects from southern tourism nostalgia to Birmingham history to children's television and children's records, among other topics. He also owns a museum of toys, advertising, holiday memorabilia and other baby boomer relics that he opens by appointment. Having lived in Birmingham his entire life, he supplies the nostalgic materials for the popular www.BirminghamRewound.com website and somehow finds time to contribute the monthly "Timepiece" column for *Birmingham* magazine.

Visit us at
www.historypress.net